D1168511

Presented to:

_____

From:

_____

Date:

_____

In the Light of the New Day

Daily Reflections *on* Finding your Purpose

Abingdon Press
Growing in Life, Serving in Faith

NASHVILLE

IN THE LIGHT OF THE NEW DAY
DAILY REFLECTIONS ON FINDING YOUR PURPOSE
Copyright © 2019 by Abingdon Press
All rights reserved.
No part of this work may be reproduced or transmitted in any form or by
any means, electronic or mechanical, including photocopying and recording,
or by any information storage or retrieval system, except as may be expressly
permitted by the 1976 Copyright Act or in writing from the publisher.
Requests for permission can be addressed to Permissions, The United
Methodist Publishing House, 2222 Rosa L. Parks Blvd., Nashville, TN,
37228-1306 or emailed to permissions@umpublishing.org.

**Library of Congress Cataloging-in-Publication Data has been
requested**

ISBN-13: 978-1-5018-8112-1

Scripture quotations are taken from the Common English Bible,
copyright 2011. Used by permission. All rights reserved.

19 20 21 22 23 24 25 26—10 9 8 7 6 5 4 3 2 1

PRINTED IN THE PEOPLE'S REPUBLIC OF CHINA

It's a Good Thing You're Here!

We know that God works all things together for good
for the ones who love God, for those who are called
according to his purpose.

—Romans 8:28

After the Potter created, he threw away the mold. You were perfect for what he designed you for and exactly what he wanted. He knew what you could do and looked forward to seeing you in action. You were created for a unique purpose.

John Henry Newman shed light on this idea when he wrote the following: "Everyone who breathes, high and low, educated and ignorant, young and old, man and woman, has a mission, has a work. We are not sent into this world for nothing. . . . God sees every one of us; He creates every soul . . . for a purpose."

He did not intend for you to wander aimlessly through life. You have a purpose every day. You have a reason for being that is bigger than your own set of goals. It's the mission you were sent here to do, and before you're beamed back up to God, you will strive to get it accomplished. He knows the distractions that will take you off the path, the trial and error that you'll go through. The thing is, he's always aware of you, always

> *J*ulfill the purpose—your mission—for which you were called, as someone who loves God.

doing what he can to keep you pointed in the right direction. He supports the work you do to fulfill the purpose for which you were born. Give him thanks and praise today.

RENEWED FOR A PURPOSE

Lord, I have a sense of mission even though I don't always know what it is I'm supposed to do. Please keep working with me, helping me discover the path that will accomplish the goal for you. Amen.

A Divine Appointment

God promised this good news about his Son ahead of time through his prophets in the Holy Scriptures. His Son was descended from David. . . . This Son is Jesus Christ our LORD. Through him we have received God's grace and our appointment to be apostles.

—Romans 1:2-5

Take a look at your business card. Is there anything that indicates who you really are? Does it mention your status at work, your mission, the reason you're here? If it doesn't you might wonder why. You are here by divine appointment to do the work of God. You have only one real boss. You have only one job to complete before you go on to your next assignment. No matter where you live, where you work, what title you list on your card, you have one real job—to do the will of God.

When did you sign up? You signed up the day you declared that Jesus was your Savior, the day you realized that the Son of God had the power to change your life. It was the best news you had ever heard. He signed the contract with you, offering to mentor you and train you for the job.

As you start your work today, stop to check in with your boss. Make sure you understand all the messages in your inbox so

> *P*ursue the job for which you signed up: to do the will of God.

you can make a difference. You're the one he named to get the job done, and he's very proud of you. It's going to be a great day.

RENEWED FOR A PURPOSE

Lord, thank you for hiring me to do the job you have in mind for me. Help me do the work you've assigned me with great love and integrity. Bless my work today in you. Amen.

The Light and the Promise

Your word is a lamp before my feet and a light
for my journey. I have sworn, and I fully mean it:
I will keep your righteous rules.

—Psalm 119:105-106

Did you ever find yourself in a situation where you felt utterly alone and in the dark? You were uncertain about the next steps, and you wondered if you would end up in dismal failure or even if you might die? It's possible in that kind of situation that you might call out to God for help, asking him to light your path and guide your next steps.

Along with that request is perhaps your bargaining position, your promise that if God does what you ask of him, you'll do something in return for him.

This psalm causes us to consider two important things. One is that you may encounter darkness at any time. You may find yourself holding on for dear life, gasping for fresh air. You may need more light for the journey at any time.

Once you're relaxed again, you need to be mindful of what happens to your thinking, what happens to your promises. You've been given a precious guide for all that happens to you through God's word, an opportunity to rest and smooth out the bumps life brings. When you rest in him, you also refuel and refresh yourself in a way that strengthens your path and allows you to carry on his work and fulfill your promises to him.

> *L*et God illuminate your way through difficult times; afterwards fulfill the promises you made.

Today, it's your day to shine for him once again.

Renewed for a Purpose

Lord, you are the oxygen, the air we breathe. Please help me shine your light wherever I am today and not wait for rough air to do so, but instead ensure the path is smooth for anyone I meet. Amen.

Because God Knows Your Name

But now, says the LORD—the one who created you, Jacob, the one who formed you, Israel: Don't fear, for I have redeemed you; I have called you by name; you are mine. When you pass through the waters, I will be with you; when through the rivers, they won't sweep over you.

—Isaiah 43:1-2

God always remembers your name. Sure, he has millions and millions of people on his roster, but somehow when it comes to you, he knows you right away. He doesn't have to slip quietly to the side and ask someone else to remind him who you are. Why? Because you are his!

When someone knows you well and has a relationship with you that is that familiar, they do their best to help you in the hard times and be with you when you might feel alone. God does that too, only he is always with you, always at your side and won't leave you alone. He wants you to hear him call your name as he puts out the welcome mat.

Scary things will come up. Hard times will hit you. You won't know what to do every time. The good news is this: God put your name in before you got there, so

Know that he has called you by name, and you may call on him for help.

he made a reservation for you to walk right up to him and let him know what is going on.

Just call on him any time you need his help.

RENEWED FOR A PURPOSE

Lord, wherever I am today, I pray that you will be near me, guiding and guarding me. Thank you for knowing my name. Amen.

God's Good Purpose for You

God is the one who enables you both to want
and to actually live out his good purposes.

—Philippians 2:13

You live and breathe and work and dance for only one reason: You have a purpose in this life. You were born to carry out a particular job for God, and he invites you every day to keep seeking that purpose. You may identify it in some way through the things you feel passionate about since God inspires your passions. You may see it through the eyes of compassion, the tears you shed on behalf of others who are in pain.

Whatever calls you, whatever rings truth in your ears so loudly it won't go away, is more than likely a piece of the puzzle, a piece of the mission and the thing you can define as your purpose. You are the only one who can actually fulfill it, the only one given that particular assignment. Oh sure, God will reassign your task if he has to, if for some reason you don't choose to complete it, but when you return home, he won't ask how many church services you attended,

he'll ask how often you attended to the needs of those around you and how many ways you found to serve others. He cheers you on even now as you seek to fulfill his

> *C*arry out the job God has invited you to complete and help those who are in need.

incredible purpose in your life. He knows you can do it.

RENEWED FOR A PURPOSE

Lord, I don't always know for sure if I'm on the right track, but I look forward to fulfilling my mission for you. Thank you for believing in me and trusting me to get it done. Amen.

Make Up Your Mind Already!

Elijah approached all the people and said,
"How long will you hobble back and forth between
two opinions? If the LORD is God, follow God.
If Baal is God, follow Baal." The people gave no answer.

—1 Kings 18:21

You may not have a split personality, but it can be pretty perplexing to be uncertain about something that really affects your life. You can waffle back and forth to such a degree that days go by, months even, and still you're on the fence, not moving forward, not going back, simply stuck in the middle somewhere.

Before we marvel at the Israelites' indecision, though, we might want to face the question squarely for ourselves. After all, how often do we get sidetracked by the current versions of Baal that exist in our world? How often do we vacillate between getting more involved with the world or following the path God intends?

Recall that Elijah challenged the prophets of Baal to prepare a sacrifice of a bull; Elijah also prepared a sacrifice. Whichever god answered with fire would be the real God. Baal did not answer. But fire fell consuming Elijah's sacrifice, and the people worshipped God.

*A*ct and take a stand to embrace your Savior in all that you do.

Realize that time slips on, and some of your choices won't present themselves to you again. on't wait for a consuming fire to make right choices.

RENEWED FOR A PURPOSE

Lord, time really does get away from me and sometimes, I'm sure, I make a mess of things when I don't handle them with your help. Let me always choose you as the most important decision I make. Amen.

The Banquet Table Awaits

All of you who are thirsty, come to the water!
Whoever has no money, come, buy food and eat!

—Isaiah 55:1

If you were invited to a fancy five-star restaurant, free of charge, no strings attached, would you go? You're not going to be pressured to buy a time-share or form a co-op, you're simply going to mingle with others and have some fabulous food, and your host will take care of it all. Well, the invitation is an open one, and you're invited every day to come to the feast. It's a standing invitation and allows you to bring friends along too if you'd like. All you have to be is a little bit thirsty.

One writer said, "I was dying of thirst. When my spiritual eyes were opened I saw the rivers of living water flowing from his pierced side. I drank of it and was satisfied. Thirst was no more. Ever since I have always drunk of that water of life, and have never been athirst in the sandy desert of this world."

God never wants you to thirst. He alone knows the way to the living waters, the place that will make your soul come alive and open the eyes of your heart. He invites you with each sunrise to come to his table, to start your day with him so that you will not thirst in the desert of this world. It's a good day to be refreshed and renewed in him. Come to the feast!

> *Come to the banquet God sets before you every day and thirst no more.*

Renewed for a Purpose

Lord, thank you for always inviting me to your table. I come with great joy and gratitude today. Amen.

The Place of Sacrifice

*All have sinned and fall short of God's glory, but all
are treated as righteous freely by his grace because of a
ransom that was paid by Christ Jesus. Through his faithfulness,
God displayed Jesus as the place of sacrifice where mercy is
found by means of his blood.*

—Romans 3:23-25

What if getting into heaven was your job? According to this Scripture,
all have sinned and have fallen short of God's glory. That means none
of us would have a free pass.

That does present a dilemma, because we like to think that we're
clever enough or smart enough, or maybe even religious enough, that
we could at least get up to the door. Unfortunately, even if we got to
the door, we might find a sign that said "Sorry, no room at the inn."

God didn't make the way back home quite that perilous. The
truth is, the way back has been taken care of and your ticket has

been purchased. All you have to do is redeem it. God alone made the sacrifice, the pure, loving, all-for-one, one-for-all sacrifice, and so we all have a way home again. Today, as you use your skills and talents to do the work you do, keep in mind this one thing: you're free. You're free to be everything you

> *Thank Jesus that his sacrifice gives you freedom to get back "home."*

can be because you have a ticket to get back home. All you have to do is pick it up and thank your Redeemer.

RENEWED FOR A PURPOSE

Lord, thank you for not leaving the ride home up to me. I know I'd never find a way to get there. Thank you for your grace and your mercy. Amen.

God's Plans for Your Good

I know the plans I have in mind for you,
declares the LORD; they are plans for peace, not disaster,
to give you a future filled with hope. When you call me
and come and pray to me, I will listen to you.
When you search for me, yes, search for me with
all your heart, you will find me.

—Jeremiah 29:11-13

When you've made your plans and filled in your to-do list, but all you accomplish is the right to watch your plans go up in smoke, or you check off just one thing on a list, it might be good to go back and remember whose you are. Go back to your Source of all that is good, get on your knees, and let him know that you've been wandering a bit too long on your own, and you really need his help. Search for him! If you do that, God promises to answer, to share the things he has in mind for you and to give you what you need. All things are possible with God, and most things are slippery slopes without him. He doesn't want you to live in fear or challenge you with one disaster after another; he simply wants you to give him your heart. He'll provide all you need from that point on.

> *S*earch for God with all your heart and he will give you all you need.

Hang this thought on the mirror of your heart today, and reflect the joy only God can give you.

RENEWED FOR A PURPOSE

Lord, thank you for bringing me back to you and for giving me hope. I look forward to all that you have planned for my life and I'm grateful. Amen.

Sharing Your Jesus

Therefore, everyone who acknowledges me
before people, I also will acknowledge before my Father
who is in heaven. But everyone who denies me before people,
I also will deny before my Father who is in heaven.

—Matthew 10:32-33

Probably most of us are comfortable sharing our faith in those settings where such discussions are natural and easy. We can talk about Jesus freely at church or at our weekly Bible study, but what about those unexpected places? What about talking about Jesus with your new friend over coffee at Starbucks or with your old friend at the football stadium?

It's hard in the same way that getting up in front of a crowd of people and making a speech is hard. It's hard because we're suddenly feeling almost naked as we reveal something about ourselves that those people might not have known about us before. We are suddenly vulnerable to their ridicule or to their assertion that religion is a private matter.

The truth for us is that God wants us to talk about him. He wants us to share the incredible gift we have in him, our future in heaven, our present opportunity

> *B*e willing to talk about God with others when you have the opportunity to do so.

for forgiveness, our sense of well-being because we have a great relationship with him.

It's okay to talk about the love of your life. You have an open invitation to do so.

RENEWED FOR A PURPOSE

Lord, you are the love of my life and I am awed by all that you do for me. Help me be willing to share what I know about you any time a good opportunity comes my way. Amen.

Before Time Began

*Their faith and this knowledge are based on
the hope of eternal life that God, who doesn't lie,
promised before time began.*

—Titus 1:2

God made a plan with love, and he did it before Genesis, before he even started speaking all things into existence. Wow! He has always known us and with that knowledge created a promise that he keeps forever: He will bring us back to himself one day and give us the hope of eternal life.

Now that we know where we're going, what difference does that make in our day today? What can we do today that we'll be pleased to share with him when we get to see him face to face? How can we show our love to someone today? We're not always conscious of our choices in light of that moment when we're talking with our Creator, but sometimes it's good to look at things from that perspective.

After all, we're finite and we're pretty good at squandering time. We know we don't have forever, and yet we don't always make our moments count. This is the day the Lord has made, and we are glad. Let's walk with him and work with him and grow in him today so that we have more faith

Make today count by walking with him and growing in knowledge and faith.

and more knowledge and more hope than we have had in years. It's your day to shine!

RENEWED FOR A PURPOSE

Lord, thank you for this new day and thanks for making plans to bring me hope and faith and the way back to you someday. Help me make today count so that I'll be glad to share my stories of today when we're standing face to face. Amen.

Let Me Give You a Hand

*Christ is just like the human body—a body is a unit
and has many parts; and all the parts of the body are
one body, even though there are many.*

—1 Corinthians 12:12

When we think of ourselves as the body of Christ, we need to remember that all the churches who worship Jesus everywhere in the world are part of that body. We're all part of the same Lord and, therefore, we're still each other's hands and feet. What affects one of us, really affects all of us.

It's the ripple effect. What happens to one member of the body has a consequence for the rest of the body. We have a love of creating labels in our culture, and we have traditions based in theology for the many churches that make up the body of Christ. One of them may be a "hand" and one may be a "leg," but each one represents the same God, the author of each of us.

Today, let's celebrate the fact that God has such a diverse body, linked together by the blood of Christ. Let's thank him for one another and the work that each church does to make the world a better place. Wherever you live, wherever you work, wherever you worship, you are an

Celebrate that you are part of the body of Christ, wherever you live, work, or worship.

important member of the body of Christ, and we need you to do the wonderful things you do to make us one. Celebrate God's love for his church today.

RENEWED FOR A PURPOSE

Lord, thank you for creating your church here on earth and for all the people who belong to you. Help us be good hands and good feet and good hearts for you, and help us serve each other well. Amen.

God's Nourishment!

The LORD's Instruction is perfect, reviving one's very being. The LORD's laws are faithful, making naive people wise. The LORD's regulations are right, gladdening the heart. The LORD's commands are pure, giving light to the eyes. Honoring the LORD is correct, lasting forever. The LORD's judgments are true.

—Psalm 19:7-9

If you're into energy drinks, you probably like that you can mix a sprinkle of this and a smidge of that, blend it with some yogurt and bananas and strawberries, and off you go for the day, fortified and energized. You have been revived.

God nourishes you in a similar way in that he is the One Source that you can go to for all your needs. When you want to learn from him, when you're ready to listen, he's there with amazing insights and new ideas. He's ready to pour out his Spirit in your direction, guiding you and giving you a new perspective. He's interested in making you brilliant so that you can be proud of your choices and become wiser in the things you do.

Honor him and praise him. Give him a chance to renew your enthusiasm so you can fulfill the life purpose he designed for you. He wants you to succeed, and he

> *T*ake in all of God's nourishment, renewed by his Spirit to accomplish his plans.

will make sure you have all you need to make that happen. Only he can truly nourish your soul!

RENEWED FOR A PURPOSE

Lord, thank you for teaching me and revitalizing me today. Help me keep my eyes open to all that you have for me, and let me shine my light for you. Amen.

Is God Still in the Building?

Certainly the faithful love of the LORD hasn't ended; certainly God's compassion isn't through! They are renewed every morning. Great is your faithfulness. I think: The LORD is my portion! Therefore, I'll wait for him.

—Lamentations 3:22-24

It's a struggle sometimes to remember that God hasn't left the building—that is, the building up of his people, the building of relationships, and the building of his church. He hasn't left us, and yet we may try to seek him the same way we'd do a celebrity sighting, hoping to catch a glimpse of him when we least expect. The writer of this Scripture reminds us that God hasn't quit, hasn't walked away from his creation, and his acts of kindness aren't done. He begins them anew every morning. Think of that! God rises with fresh thoughts of love, not tainted by yesterday, not carried on as leftovers, but new and fresh and ready to be delivered to his children.

What does it mean that the Lord is our portion? If my portion is God, that means he's everything I get. He's my whole, my life, my breath and spirit. If I recall every morning with the rising of the sun that he is there, ready to feed me and renew me and shower me with grace, then I receive the portion he meant for me to have.

> *W*ait for God who renews you every morning with his love and compassion.

RENEWED FOR A PURPOSE

Lord, thank you for giving me your kindness and your goodness every single day in fresh and loving ways. Help me take your love with me wherever I go today. Amen.

That's Not My Job!

If I, your LORD and teacher, have washed your feet, you too must wash each other's feet. I have given you an example: just as I have done, you also must do. I assure you, servants aren't greater than their master, nor are those who are sent greater than the one who sent them. Since you know these things, you will be happy if you do them.

—John 13:14-17

Unfortunately, the idea that something is "not my job" has permeated every area of life. The server at the restaurant doesn't bring the water because that's the hostess's job. The person on the street corner doesn't pick up the trash and put it in the bin because that's the street cleaner's job.

The little things we could do, and most of the time could do pretty easily, end up not being done because we've got the not-my-job disease. So today, remind yourself that you are always invited to do the job, whatever it is, as soon as you see the need or have the opportunity. You can wash the feet of others just as easily as you can be served by them.

Your job is always changing and your work for the Lord is always ongoing. If you think it's somebody else's job, give that another thought today and lead on!

> *S*erve by helping others, doing the little things, even though it may not be in your "job description."

RENEWED FOR A PURPOSE

Lord, thank you for reminding me that I have the job to be aware of others and their needs and that I can pick up the baton and move forward to get things done no matter how big or small the job may be. Amen.

Come to the Party!

There are different spiritual gifts but the same Spirit;
and there are different ministries and the same Lord; and there
are different activities but the same God who produces all of
them in everyone. A demonstration of the Spirit is given to each
person for the common good.

—1 Corinthians 12:4-7

When God invited you to his party, he already had in mind just what you could bring. He knew what you'd be good at and what talents you could share with others. He knew your personality style and who else would be there who might need time just with you. He gave you everything you need to enjoy yourself immensely.

Your gifts and talents are fabulous, but if you stay in your house and never come out, very few people will ever get to appreciate them. You can be wonderful in isolation, but you were made for community. You're a piece of somebody else's puzzle. Somebody else holds a piece of your puzzle. It works that way because we're meant to be interconnected, sharing what we have and what God has blessed us with for the good of us all.

Show up at God's party so that you can provide a blessing to others and be blessed by others.

Every day we're invited to share our talents and offer seeds of wisdom so that God's love will flourish everywhere. Keep blossoming.

RENEWED FOR A PURPOSE

Lord, thank you for your standing invitation to come and share the many gifts you've given me. Help me bless others as you have blessed me. Amen.

Still Calling His Followers

As Jesus walked alongside the Galilee Sea, he saw two brothers . . . throwing fishing nets into the sea. . . . "Come, follow me," he said, "and I'll show you how to fish for people."

—Matthew 4:18-19

If Jesus stopped by any of our towns today to call his followers, would he venture into the heart of commerce? Would he go to Wall Street and look for the biggest investment gurus or set his sights on a physician from the local hospital? It's interesting to try to imagine who he might deem to be worthy disciples, and yet one thing is clear: You would be on his list. He would call you to follow him. Today, more than anything else, he wants to help you cast a bigger vision for your life, fill your nets to overflowing with the good things of God, and help to heal your wounds in any possible way. Jesus is still calling.

If you're already following him, think for a moment how that affects your daily decisions, your daily purpose. How do you align yourself with his will for your life? How often do you truly allow him to lead?

Of course, the trouble with followers sometimes is that they try to scoot ahead of their leaders, sometimes taking a wrong trail. Wherever you are today, pause a moment and reflect on who is leading your life. Are you following Jesus even now?

> *R*espond to the calling of Jesus, letting him guide you as you become a fisher of souls.

Renewed for a Purpose

Lord, as I go about my business today, help me seek your guidance and direction. Help me be a wise and loving follower. Amen.

Do You Have the Right Equipment?

May the God of peace, who brought back the
great shepherd of the sheep, our LORD Jesus,
from the dead by the blood of the eternal covenant,
equip you with every good thing to do his will,
by developing in us what pleases him through Jesus Christ.
To him be the glory forever and always.

—Hebrews 13:20-21

Whenever you start a new task or a new job, it's always a good idea to check to be sure you have what you need to get the job done.

Our work for God is somewhat similar. He calls us and then he equips us to get the job done. We don't always know what we'll need so we have to rely on him for the proper equipment.

You don't know where you'll be or who you might be with when you suddenly realize a tool is missing, something that might have helped you be more effective. Perhaps you need more experience with a certain kind of person, so that you know how to handle people like that in the future. It's all about learning.

As St. Augustine said, "Since you cannot do good to all, you are to pay special regard to those who, by the accidents of time, or place, or circumstances, are brought into closer connection with you."

> *C*ontinue to add spiritual tools so that you can do good to those who cross your path.

When those things happen, you need to be prepared. May God continue to keep your toolbox full.

RENEWED FOR A PURPOSE

Lord, only you know the people I'll meet and what kind of information I'll need to be an effective witness for you. Please guide me and equip me as only you can so I'm always ready to do good. Amen.

Happy Birthday!

Even if our bodies are breaking down on the outside, the person that we are on the inside is being renewed every day.

—2 Corinthians 4:16

Okay, so it may not be your literal birthday today, but every day that you wake up refreshed in the spirit, ready to get going, you experience a kind of rebirth. After all, our job on earth is about waking up to what is real, waking up to our awareness of God and the beauty of a spirit-filled life. Our bodies may well have to deal with breaking down, but no matter how many candles are on our cakes, we are building up for our trip home to the embrace of our heavenly Parent.

So rise and shine, birthday person! It's your day to keep growing and learning and becoming more of what God has in mind for you. It's an exciting journey, and each day brings a discovery of something you might not have realized before. You have been kind of sleepy, you know, and it never hurts to stretch a little so you can wake up more fully.

What will you do today to celebrate your birthday? What light can you add to the world that will awaken the spirit of even one other person? Go ahead, add

> *W*ake up to the beauty of a spirit-filled life, becoming what God has in mind for you.

a candle, sing a song of praise, and get out there. The world needs you today to join in the celebration.

RENEWED FOR A PURPOSE

Lord, help me wake up to you in every possible way. Lead me into the paths of others who struggle to see you in a better and more consistent light. Amen.

Finding the Superhero in You

Therefore, imitate God like dearly loved children.
Live your life with love, following the example of Christ,
who loved us and gave himself for us.
You were once in darkness, but now you are light in the LORD,
so live your life as children of light. Light produces fruit that
consists of every sort of goodness, justice, and truth.

—Ephesians 5:1-2; 8-9

Don't you love watching children at play when they are pretending to be superheroes? The superheroes don their capes and vow to protect the innocent, always ready to defend and fight for the right. They definitely make the world a safer place.

We can't really pretend to be God, but we can imitate those traits that we recognize as being a part of his holiness.

We can follow the examples that we have recorded in Scripture of what it means to love others as we love ourselves. We have biblical heroes who serve the people of God and who serve as examples for us to follow.

Today, "pretend" to be a little kinder, a little more generous, and a little more conscious of God's great love than you were the day before. Chances

> *I*mitate Jesus today by being a little kinder and a little more generous to those around you.

are, it won't be long before it's not a pretense at all, but the truth of who you are.

RENEWED FOR A PURPOSE

Lord, help me today to try to walk further in your shoes. Help me lean into you so much that I can show your love and your light to everyone I meet. Amen.

Time to Blossom and Bear Fruit

*I am the vine; you are the branches. If you remain in me and
I in you, then you will produce much fruit. . . . If you
remain in me and my words remain in you, ask for
whatever you want and it will be done for you. My Father
is glorified when you produce much fruit and in this way prove
that you are my disciples.*

—John 15:5, 7-8

If you've ever had a garden, even a container garden on your city patio, you recognize that it takes more than just a passing interest in your plants to make sure they grow. Actually, it takes a fair amount of attention from you to make sure the soil is properly prepared and the right nutrients have been applied. You have to check to see if your plant will thrive better in the sun or the shade, and then you're off to find the watering can. So far, you've done a lot of work, but nothing has happened. You set the groundwork, but the rest is out of your hand.

It's kind of that way with your faith too. Jesus is the vine and when you came to faith in him, you became a branch on his tree, rooted in his soil and ready to grow according to his will and favor. Without him, you would wither up and die because no matter what you do, you can't grow on your own. As with the plant in your garden, attention needs to be paid in the right ways for growth to happen.

> *T*hrive where you are because Jesus, the vinedresser, provides all that you need to grow.

Each time you seek the Son, you begin to stretch more toward him, growing in his light and love.

RENEWED FOR A PURPOSE

Lord, thank you for nurturing me and guiding me so that I can grow stronger in you. Amen.

Love, Prayers, and Enemies!

You have heard that it was said, You must love your neighbor and hate your enemy. But I say to you, love your enemies and pray for those who harass you so that you will be acting as children of your Father who is in heaven.

—Matthew 5:43-45

There are days when we might wonder why the "bad guys" seem to keep finding a way to succeed in the world, while we hang on for dear life. Then along comes this Scripture from Jesus telling us to pray for those bad guys and even love them because that's what God wants from us.

God makes it bright and cheery for everyone regardless of how he is treated, and he expects us to do the same.

Wow! There's a little show-stopping thought! Why does God treat everyone the same? Ah, perhaps it is that he can only do good. He only knows how to love so that's what he offers.

How about us? What if we didn't have an ounce of hate or jealousy or unkindness in our bodies? We'd probably be a little closer to our Father because then we'd pray and love and offer our hearts to everyone, friends and enemies alike. All who see us would see his face for exactly what it is—the face of love.

> *A*s a child of God, pray for those who do not act with honor or kindness or love.

Let's pray for those who annoy us, challenge us, and most of all need us to help them find the God of love today.

RENEWED FOR A PURPOSE

Lord, I have to admit I don't always understand how life works, or even how to tell the bad guys from the good guys. Help me be on the side of good, though, according to your will and purpose. Amen.

Refreshing Rains

If we live by the Spirit, let's follow the Spirit. Let's not become arrogant, make each other angry, or be jealous of each other.

—Galatians 5:25-26

As we follow the Spirit, breathe in the Spirit and are filled by the Spirit, we are more prepared to embrace the gifts of the Spirit. Arrogance, anger, and jealousy have a chance to be replaced with more godly virtues such as patience, kindness, goodness, and self-control.

If you want to follow the Spirit more closely today, invite him in to your daily routine, asking him to bless your home, your work, and your heart. Listen for his urging when he suggests that it's time to pray or time to relax. Thank him for giving you the incredible peace and comfort and sense of connection you feel with God's Word and with your faith.

You're bathed in the Spirit as surely as if you were swimming in a small pond or floating in a great ocean. You're awash with his presence and grace and made whole again. You simply have to create the opportunity for him to come into your awareness.

Today, relax with the Spirit of God and receive the gifts of faithfulness and love, joy and peace. Be his voice, his arms, his opportunity to speak with

> *I*nvite the Spirit of God into your daily routine, listening to his voice and acting accordingly.

someone who may yet long for his embrace.

RENEWED FOR A PURPOSE

Lord, I invite your Holy Spirit into my life, my heart, my work, and all that I am and all that I do today in Jesus' name. Amen.

Shaking off the Dust

Like a parent feels compassion for their children—that's how the
LORD feels compassion for those who honor him. Because God
knows how we're made, God remembers we're just dust.

—Psalm 103:13-14

No doubt, we all appreciate the idea that God is compassionate about his children. He watches over each of us with great interest and concern for our well-being. Like a good parent, he sometimes lets us go out on our own. He sees every step we take, lifts us up again when we fall, and brushes off the dust when we stumble.

In the same way, he wants us to see each other with merciful eyes. He did not put us here to judge another person's way of life or someone else's looks. He did not ask us to determine right and wrong except for the choices we make for ourselves. No, what he wants is for us to go out into our neighborhoods or sit down to the dinner table with our families and remember one thing: we're all dust. We're a creation of God's hands, and we live because of his great love for us.

When we can see each other through compassionate hearts, we see the whole person, the whole possibility, the reason God is her or his Father as well as ours. Let your compassionate heart enrich the lives of everyone around you now.

> *S*erve by helping others, doing the little things, even though it may not be in your "job description."

RENEWED FOR A PURPOSE

Lord, help me have a kind heart toward all your children. Amen.

Struggles of the Heart

Little children, let's not love with words or speech
but with action and truth. This is how we will know
that we belong to the truth and reassure our hearts in
God's presence. Even if our hearts condemn us,
God is greater than our hearts and knows all things.

—1 John 3:18-20

Your heart is a critic. It reminds you when you miss an opportunity, when you don't do well, or when you fall flat on your face. It's relentless! It may even keep you from trying to do good. It can make you believe that your contribution is meaningless and that no one really needs the things you do.

But God is greater than your heart's critic.

He sees the effort you make over and over again, and he is thrilled with you. He knows you, and he loves you, and today he wants you to trust that your purpose is great in his eyes. This is your day to do one small thing with great love, and when you do your heart will soar. God designed you for good, and he loves to see your heart take wing. Do something that will make him proud today!

Do one good thing today and know that God values your contribution.

Renewed for a Purpose

Lord, I don't always feel like I'm making much of a contribution to the world or even to the people around me. Help me stop judging myself so much and keep believing that the little things I do mean a lot to you. Amen.

Invisible Means of Support

If you love me, you will keep my commandments.
I will ask the Father, and he will send another Companion, who
will be with you forever. This Companion is the Spirit
of Truth, whom the world can't receive because it neither
sees him nor recognizes him. You know him, because
he lives with you and will be with you.

—John 14:15-17

In an effort to look reality squarely in the face, we sometimes overlook another reality, the very supernatural reality that is part of being a believer. God is spirit, and as well as operating with us physically as we wander about in our temporal bodies, he also works on our spirits. We work on our spirits too, praying to be faithful, hoping to be more like the One who created us.

It's natural for God to talk with us about recognizing his Spirit that he placed within us. He knows we are finite. He knows we are human. The only real hope we have, then, is that the incredible human spirit he gave us will mix and mingle with the Holy Spirit he also gave us. He knew we couldn't get through life without an invisible means of support. He sent a Companion, the Spirit of Truth, to live with us on a full-time basis.

Give thanks for God sending his Spirit of Truth that we may be comforted and instructed.

A companion, any companion, is someone that you love to pal around with. You may not think of the Spirit of Truth as that kind of companion, but as you reflect on that today, get a little closer to him and thank him for all he does to help you navigate your walk here on earth.

Renewed for a Purpose

Lord, I am amazed that you would give such a glorious part of yourself to me, to live with me and teach me and comfort me. I love you and thank you for your beautiful Spirit. Amen.

The Running Stream and the Rock

Don't you know that all the runners in the stadium run,
but only one gets the prize? So run to win. Everyone who
competes practices self-discipline in everything. The runners do
this to get a crown of leaves that shrivel up and die,
but we do it to receive a crown that never dies.

—1 Corinthians 9:24-25

In a confrontation between a stream and a rock, the stream always wins. It doesn't win through strength or might, it simply wins because it perseveres. Perhaps if we take this thought a bit further, we might see that even though the rock is solid and holding its own, it's also standing still. We might assume the rock would win simply because it looks more intimidating. But that isn't so. Sometimes in life, we're like the rock. Other times, we're the stream.

We spend our days trying to win at something. It's good to set goals, even if there's only one prize. Like the stream, we keep moving, being a part of the process, and flowing past the obstacles to create fresh opportunities. When we do that, regardless of where we come into the flow, or who notices our achievement, we win. God sees our efforts and rewards our self-discipline. He serves as our Rock, our steadfast and worthy

> *P*ersevere, keep running, and practice self-discipline on your way to God's prize.

prize, and he gives us the stream of grace to keep getting closer to his throne.

RENEWED FOR A PURPOSE

Lord, I know that I am not always willing to move to get things done. Sometimes I'm more like the rock and I just let things pass me by. Help me move today like a persistent stream so I get a little closer to the goals you've set for me. Amen.

Think About What You're Thinking About!

Therefore, submit to God. Resist the devil, and he will run away from you. Come near to God, and he will come near to you. Wash your hands, you sinners. Purify your hearts, you double-minded. Cry out in sorrow, mourn, and weep! Let your laughter become mourning and your joy become sadness. Humble yourselves before the LORD, and he will lift you up.

—James 4:7-10

In the stillness and the quiet hours, we find ourselves awake and poised, ready to learn more of what God would have for us. We listen carefully, desiring above all else to submit to his will.

The noise of the world occupies our minds. It is the work of the evil one that you should not realize how little time you spend in prayer and contemplation. He's a wily one, after all, cunning and deceitful, and all you have to do to get him to flee is resist him.

Resist him and he will run from you. He runs because the closer you get to God the less he can stand the company you keep. So watch what you're thinking, what you're listening to, and what you're perceiving as real. Wait in the stillness for the voice of the One who loves you more than life itself. He alone can lift you up over all the noise.

> *B*e mindful of the company you keep, the thoughts you harbor, and the things you watch.

Renewed for a Purpose

Lord, it is often noisy inside my head. I know that I need to quiet the stress and the anxiety that hover around me, waiting to take over when my spirit is weak. I submit myself to you and to your love for me. Amen.

Living Out Your Purpose

Therefore, my loved ones, just as you always obey me, not
just when I am present but now even more while I am away,
carry out your own salvation with fear and
trembling. God is the one who enables you both to want
and to actually live out his good purposes.

—Philippians 2:12-13

When Rick Warren wrote his life-changing book, *The Purpose Driven Life*, he helped us develop an awareness of how important our relationship with God is.

God designed us intentionally, and he alone knows what he has called us to do. No amount of self-searching will get us to the answer.

You may still be hoping to discover your life purpose, feeling slightly off center, somewhat less than fulfilled in your current career. If something is nagging you, causing you to be uncomfortable, urging you to shift your attention in a new direction, then today is a good day to stop and listen. Today is the day to go back to your Father for clear guidance and direction.

As Albert Einstein once said, "The life of an individual only has meaning insofar as it aids in making the life of every

*F*ollow God's guidance and direction to discover your good purpose in life.

living thing nobler and more beautiful. Life is sacred, that is to say, it is the supreme value to which all other values are subordinate."

RENEWED FOR A PURPOSE

Lord, thank you for loving me so much and for designing me for a very real purpose. Help me keep coming back to you for guidance until the way is clear. Amen.

Finding Just the Right Recipe

A person will harvest what they plant. Those who plant only for their own benefit will harvest devastation from their selfishness, but those who plant for the benefit of the Spirit will harvest eternal life from the Spirit.

—Galatians 6:7-8

Culturally, we're all about individuals. We elevate self-indulgence, self-satisfaction, self-esteem. Of course, sometimes what we get back from those are things we're not so pleased with—self-loathing and self-righteousness come to mind. Though being a strong individual, one who can be counted on and respected, is a good thing; the call to most of us is about stepping aside from the self and looking out for the other person.

We've been planted on this earth for a reason, and part of that reason is about spreading the seeds of God's love, watering the tender plants someone else started, and helping to distribute the fruit of our labors. From there, we can create all kinds of recipes—a cookbook—for good living.

Today, then, our job is to wave the self aside and discover what we can do to benefit at least one other person. You may not have the perfect recipe for doing

> *S*tepping aside from your self-interest, discover what you can do to help someone else today.

good, but you have all the ingredients. You got them the day you signed up to live in God's garden. It's your day to bloom.

RENEWED FOR A PURPOSE

Lord, I get so caught up in what I'm doing, I sometimes forget that you've put me in the midst of a lot of people who need to know you better. Give me the wisdom to help in ways that please you. Amen.

Spiritual Muscle Fatigue

Dear friend, I'm praying that all is well with you
and that you enjoy good health in the same way
that you prosper spiritually.

—3 John 2

How are your spiritual muscles today? Are they fatigued by all the working out you've been doing the past few days or are they somewhat limp from a lack of use, somewhat less developed than they might be?

Your health is good when it is good emotionally and spiritually as well as physically. You can run five miles every morning and eat a lot of whole grains and raw vegetables and still feel somewhat fatigued, somewhat disconnected to your heart. If that's the case, take a look at the last time you ran the race for the prize that never perishes, fought the good fight for all that pleases your Creator, and managed to exercise your privilege to worship any way that you choose.

Add to that the spiritual food that comes from the fruit of the Spirit and the living waters of Jesus. Nourish yourself with kindness and goodness, as well as self-control and see if your muscles don't feel stronger, your smile brighter, and your day happier.

> *Nourish yourself with the fruit of the Spirit, practicing kindness, goodness, and self-control.*

Tap into God's training program and really develop your spiritual muscles. They will sustain you and keep you strong all the days of your life.

RENEWED FOR A PURPOSE

Lord, I know I don't exercise nearly as much as I should either physically or spiritually. Help me strengthen myself in you. Amen.

What Have You Done for Me Lately?

"When did we see you sick or in prison and visit you?" Then the king will reply to them, "I assure you that when you have done it for one of the least of these brothers and sisters of mine, you have done it for me."

—Matthew 25:39-40

Some days we are overwhelmed with life, and we can barely take care of ourselves. Giving to others doesn't come up on our radar. We don't put ourselves out of the way. If we're lucky, though, God will put someone in our path who is in greater need than we are. He will help us to see that we still have something to give and that we're still in his care and keeping as well. That one person will remind us that we may not be able to take on a whole load of people, but we can take on at least the one who is in need.

Mother Teresa said, "If you can't feed a hundred people, then feed just one." Feeding one person may simply mean offering a kind word or a smile. It may mean helping them get a seat on a crowded bus. It can mean many things, but each time you respond, each time you say yes to

> *F*ind one person today and offer a kind word and a smile, or offer to meet a physical need.

helping another person, you say yes to God. He sees what you do and rewards you for it.

It's a great day to do something good. What will you do?

RENEWED FOR A PURPOSE

Lord, you have blessed me and I am grateful. Help me bless others in any way that I can today. Amen.

Proclaiming the Year of the Lord's Favor

He unrolled the scroll and found the place where it was written: The Spirit of the LORD is upon me, because the LORD has anointed me. He has sent me to preach good news to the poor, to proclaim release to the prisoners and recovery of sight to the blind, to liberate the oppressed, and to proclaim the year of the LORD's favor. He rolled up the scroll, gave it back to the synagogue assistant, and sat down. Every eye in the synagogue was fixed on him. He began to explain to them, "Today, this scripture has been fulfilled just as you heard it."

—Luke 4:17-21

As you unroll the scroll of the new day, remember all the assignments Jesus was given when he came to earth. As the Savior, he was ready to serve God in every way. Delivering the good news and healing the sick were just part of it. One of the outstanding aspects of his ministry was that he could proclaim the year of God's favor. He could tell a starving world that the Bread of Life would be with them forevermore. Jesus fulfilled his mission using all that was available to him. He was our living example of what it means to be filled with the Spirit.

> *F*ulfill the mission to love the Lord completely and to love one another as well.

So what does he want from us? What work are we here to do? Perhaps we could discover just one idea—to love. Imagine if we fulfilled the mission to love the Lord with all our heart and mind and soul and to love one another as well.

RENEWED FOR A PURPOSE

Lord, keep my mind and heart open to your leading. Thanks for empowering me to do your work. Amen.

Simply Because You Are Faithful

*All you who are faithful, love the L*ORD*! The L*ORD
*protects those who are loyal, but he pays the proud back to
the fullest degree. All you who wait for the L*ORD*,
be strong and let your heart take courage.*

—Psalm 31:23-24

Loyalty and faithfulness seem like archaic words these days. We seldom see them in action. Companies are not loyal to their workers even after years of service. Friends are not loyal to each other. So how do we become loyal and faithful to those we've made a commitment to, and especially to God?

Remember that faithfulness is not really a goal or a destination, but a manner of traveling. It's the thing we always carry with us. It's packed with power when it serves in little ways. We are faithful in little things all the time. Mother Teresa said she did not pray to be successful, she prayed to be faithful—a good prayer for any of us. There are many biblical stories of those who were faithful in small matters being elevated then to watch over greater things. Even when the job was no longer pleasant, even when it was fearful, even unto death, Jesus remained faithful.

> *C*ontinue in your faithfulness that you may experience his strength and protection.

As his children, we are directed to complete the mission God gave us. His work cannot be done without our faithful willingness to continue to do it. He protects, strengthens, and supports all we do in his name because we are faithful.

RENEWED FOR A PURPOSE

Father, thank you for being the anchor to my life, the steadfast support, and the one I can always trust to be there. I treasure your loyalty to me and pray I will always be loyal to you in return. Amen.

Bring on the Love

Dear friends, let's love each other, because love is from God, and everyone who loves is born from God and knows God.

—1 John 4:7

When it comes to love, we're all merely students. We must sit at the feet of the Master. God has loved us beyond measure; he has given his Son for us and provided for our well-being, and yet we still are fledglings. We look to him to help us understand the grace, the forgiveness, and the divinity of love, for we cannot create it ourselves. He is the sun and we are just reflections of his light.

St. Francis de Sales wrote, "You learn to speak by speaking, to study by studying, to run by running, to work by working; and just so you learn to love God and man by loving."

We have an assignment. Let's begin today by doing the things that help us learn more about what it means to love others. Let's get out our notebooks and jot down some little things we can do to become better at the art of love. We must study diligently, listen attentively, and practice, practice, practice. Then we must observe our own results to see just how far we've come.

> *P*ractice love. Practice love. Practice Love. Thereby you show your love for God.

Loving others is easy when they are nearby and love us in return. Loving others also urges us forward when we hear of natural disasters or neighbors in need. Loving each other is a mission. God has set each one of us on that mission no matter where we are.

RENEWED FOR A PURPOSE

Lord, you have loved me in more ways than I can ever understand. You have given me everything I need. Help me be generous and loving to those around me. Amen.

And Then She Said . . .

Without wood a fire goes out; without gossips,
conflict calms down.

—Proverbs 26:20

Nothing spreads faster than a little gossip. It's amazing how often we fuel the flames of someone else's misfortune or someone's unwise decisions. We get involved in office chatter or neighborhood smoke and don't even really know why we do it. What is it that makes us so willing to keep someone else's misery alive and well through our participation in such conversation?

What God wants is for us to be kind, always kind. If being kind means you gently turn aside from the gossips in your neighborhood, then so be it.

Gossip can destroy someone. It rarely lifts them up. If we go back to 1 Corinthians 13 and look at what we are admonished to remember about love, then we can determine how to handle something like gossip. It reminds us that "love is patient, love is kind, it isn't jealous, it doesn't brag, it isn't arrogant, it isn't rude, it doesn't seek its own advantage, it isn't irritable, it doesn't keep a record of complaints, it isn't happy with injustice," and we might add, it doesn't listen to gossip.

> *Refuse to be drawn into gossip; instead, respond with patience and kindness.*

Today is a good day to be kind and to love. That is the path to all that is good.

Renewed for a Purpose

Lord, help me recognize when I need to pass on listening to the conversations that hurt others. Help me be strong in you and be kind in all I do. Amen.

In the Reflection of Your Attitude

*Who among you will give your children a stone
when they ask for bread? Or give them a snake when
they ask for fish? If you who are evil know how
to give good gifts to your children, how much more
will your heavenly father give good things
to those who ask him. Therefore, you should treat people
in the same way that you want people to treat you.*

—Matthew 7:9-12

When we come at the world with a nasty disposition, somewhat like Scrooge before his change of heart, we often find the world treats us with a nasty disposition as well. When we arrive with smiles on our faces and open hearts, we usually get matching receptions.

The pattern of our friendships matches that of our relationship with God. When we approach God with the intention of getting to know him better and drawing near to him with love and gratitude, we show him what we want from him too. We've let him know that a relationship with him is important to us.

Step back to see how people respond to you today. If the response is not the one you want, then help people look at you in a new way. Help them treat

> *R*espond to people you meet today with an openness and warmth— see if it pays off.

you better by giving them the best you have to offer. Giving them your best is easier to do when you remember all the good gifts your heavenly father has given you.

RENEWED FOR A PURPOSE

Lord, please be with me today and help me learn more about how to build our relationship. Help me also give my best self to those you have put in my path. Amen.

So Close and yet so Far!

God made the nations so they would seek him, perhaps even reach out to him and find him. In fact, God isn't far away from any of us. In God we live, move, and exist. As some of your own poets said, "We are his offspring."

—Acts 17:27-28

You've probably had moments in your spiritual walk where you thought God was so close you could touch his hand or feel his presence. You were elated to know that the God of the Universe was willing to come whenever you reached out for him.

What is it then that causes us to shift our bearings, sometimes so much that we can hardly sense the Spirit no matter how hard we try?

The answer may lie in the fact that we as his children continue to wander off on our own, forgetting where home is. We get lost in insignificant things and give them more power than they deserve.

We make our own gods just like the Israelites did. We are just like they were.

We live and move and have our being in the God of the Universe. Without him we are only dust blown around by the winds of confusion. We are

> *R*eturn to God and his strength if you feel you've wandered off a bit— it's a new day.

without the strength to withstand the world's pressures. With him, we can do all things.

Give thanks and praise to the one who lives in you and around you in every moment. Reach out in love and joy to him!

RENEWED FOR A PURPOSE

Lord, it's a new day and I am in great need of you. Help me see you at every turn and let others see you through me. Help me be worthy of being called your child. Amen.

Cheering You On

*And let us consider each other carefully for the purpose
of sparking love and good deeds. Don't stop meeting together
with other believers, which some people have gotten
into the habit of doing. Instead, encourage each other,
especially as you see the day drawing near.*

—Hebrews 10:24-25

Isn't it wonderful to have a champion? Someone who cheers you on and encourages your dreams and your life direction. They see the real you. They hope and pray for you, and they help you keep going. They are the wind beneath your wings as they help you reach goals.

You have an eternal champion in Jesus Christ. He is always ready to cheer you on and to remind you of your goal. He's always interested in the things you do and in the friendships you build because he's all about relationship. After all, it's difficult to love your neighbor as yourself if you don't know your neighbor.

Whatever you do today, remember to have your radar set on high to connect in every good way with the people around you.

Cheer them on and bless their work. Help them to know that what they do matters not just to them, but to you, and even more so, to God. We'll all succeed if we pull together!

> *S*et your mind to encouraging others in their work, letting them know they matter.

Renewed for a Purpose

Lord, help me recognize those moments when I can be a cheerleader for someone else. Help me plant the seeds of your love anywhere I can today. Amen.

Watching Out for the Other Guy

Everything is permitted, but everything isn't beneficial.
Everything is permitted, but everything doesn't build others up.
No one should look out for their own advantage, but they should
look out for each other.

—1 Corinthians 10:23-24

We're inclined to think that we can do whatever we want as long as it doesn't hurt someone else. That may not be a bad rule of thumb, but it doesn't help us become more caring for others.

Paul's comments to the Corinthians were aimed at getting them to be more mindful of one another, to make it a practice to watch out for the other guy. We all appreciate it when someone takes us under her or his wing and takes care of something we need, offering us a helping hand, a gift of food or a place to stay. The outcome of this generous behavior is that both people benefit, the giver and the receiver.

As you go about your life today, pay attention to those in your care, who need what you do for them, who benefit from your attention. The more you offer them a hand, the more God will bless your efforts. He sees your heart and applauds the good things that you do.

Give and receive with grace and thankfulness because doing so benefits everyone.

RENEWED FOR A PURPOSE

Lord, help me be more aware of the needs of those around me. Help me open my heart and my hands and let me genuinely minister to the needs of others. Amen.

It's All Good!

Comfort the discouraged. Help the weak. Be patient with everyone. Make sure no one repays a wrong with a wrong, but always pursue the good for each other and everyone else.

—1 Thessalonians 5:14-15

God pursued what was good right from the beginning. He looked at each step of his creation and declared it to be good. He was pleased when he finished his work because he could truthfully say, "It's all good!"

Generally, we try to see the good in a situation. We may dismiss those parts that don't feel quite as good as the rest and simply declare that it's all okay. The truth for us, though, is that we have to actually do just what God did: We have to pursue what is good. It doesn't just come to us. In fact, we often encounter things that are somewhat muddy, things in need of an overhaul. We're given those things so we can shine a light on them and bring the good out of them.

If you haven't been called a "do-gooder" in a while, you might want to reconsider the things you pursue. You don't need your good works to be noticed, though, you simply need to know that you're doing all you can to make a difference, even if it's only for one other person. Keep working at it

> *Dare to be called a "do-gooder" because you pursue right and honorable things.*

until you can step back and honestly say, "It's all good."

Renewed for a Purpose

Lord, help me do the kind of good you want me to do. Sometimes I intend to do good things, but I get caught up in my own day and discover at the end of it, I didn't take time to reach out to anyone else. Help me always pursue the good in myself and others. Amen.

More Than a Fig Tree

Jesus responded, "I assure you that if you have faith and don't doubt, you will not only do what was done to the fig tree. You will even say to this mountain, 'Be lifted up and thrown into the lake.' And it will happen. If you have faith, you will receive whatever you pray for."

—Matthew 21:21-22

When Jesus was hungry and found the fig tree without fruit, he spoke to it and caused it to wither and die. He reprimanded it for not bearing fruit as it should. It was a wonderful metaphor for what God expects of his children, but it was also a lesson for his followers. It was a lesson about faith. How do we get to the place where our ability to suspend doubt is so strong that we can speak and the things of nature will respond? For most of us, getting a mountain to rise up and throw itself into the lake, or speaking to the storm and getting it to calm down, are experiences we don't expect to ever have. We simply don't have that kind of faith.

Perhaps what we have to recognize is that we still are followers with very weak faith. We're not much further along than the disciples were when it comes to completely understanding and trusting the power of God that is unleashed in real faith.

Have the faith to totally trust God so that your life will make a miraculous difference.

As you venture out into a new day, examine your faith. Imagine trusting and believing so much that your faith could move mountains or even wither a fig tree.

RENEWED FOR A PURPOSE

Lord, I know I have weak faith. I ask you to keep working with me to help me see you in ways that strengthen and renew my faith in every area of my life. Amen.

How Many Terabytes Is That?

This is the disciple who testifies concerning these things and who wrote them down. We know that his testimony is true. Jesus did many other things as well. If all of them were recorded, I imagine the world itself wouldn't have enough room for the scrolls that would be written.

—John 21:24-25

Imagine trying to record all that Jesus did and then running it on a computer program. Let's say you could give him a trillion bytes of space. Would that be enough? Would you have enough space left to capture the story of his life on earth, not to mention the stories of the lives he touches today?

As believers we're still giving testimony to the things we've seen and done because of the life and death and resurrection of Jesus. We're still standing in his light and sharing his heart with others every waking day.

We do this by living the best life we can and working to be a good sermon. We're walking stories of what faith is all about.

Are you aware of moments when you shared your faith lately? Sometimes you are when you share with someone who still struggles to believe, and you can

> *W*rite your faith story in such a way that others will read and be moved closer to God.

tell you've opened the door a little, giving that person more to think about and causing them to want to hear more. Those are fabulous moments and make your heart rejoice.

If you're doing your part, someone is reading your faith story with every encounter they have with you. Make it a good one.

RENEWED FOR A PURPOSE

Lord, I know I don't always think about how well I'm telling your story. Help me be aware of all the ways I can help someone else see your light. Amen.

To Know God Is to Love God

The person who doesn't love does not know God,
because God is love. This is how the love of God
is revealed to us: God has sent his only Son into the
world so that we can live through him.

—1 John 4: 8-9

Remember a song written by Phil Spector called "To Know Him Is to Love Him"? It's actually a great song to sing to God. Whenever you feel his presence and sense his smile on your life, it makes everything worthwhile. It's your turn to smile back because nothing is better than that.

Once you finish singing your heart out to God, then take the next step. Start seeing the people that you love already as people you could also sing that song to. After you've sung to all the people you know well, then look at people you work with who also need more love and change up the song for them. Then, take a giant leap and see if you can sing the song to your enemies. That's right. See if you can put in the name of someone you don't especially feel fond of, but someone that Jesus died for just the same as he did for you.

> *L*ove each other—family, friends, and enemies!—proving you are a child born of God.

God wants you to love others. He wants you to love your families and your friends and those you don't even know yet. He wants you to love everyone he loves. He has a very big Christmas card list. See if you can love others with his heart today.

Renewed for a Purpose

Lord, thank you for loving me. Give me the insight, the desire, and the ability to love others the way you love me. Amen.

Opening the Eyes of Your Heart

I pray that the God of our LORD Jesus Christ,
the Father of glory, will give you a spirit of wisdom and
revelation that makes God known to you. I pray that
the eyes of your heart will have enough light to see what is
the hope of God's call, what is the richness of God's
glorious inheritance among believers.

—Ephesians 1:17-18

The light comes flooding in. As the room gets brighter, you can see everything that it contains. You can see the beautiful tapestries, the delicate floral prints, the incredible furnishings. It's an amazing sight and you're part of it. It's beyond any richness you ever imagined.

This little imaginary journey has just been presented to you by the God of all glory, the one who has an amazing inheritance to bestow upon his children. Your eyes have been opened and the light has dawned.

As a believer, you know that God's storehouses are full. His faithfulness is steadfast and his ability to lavish his love on you is without comparison. All that he needs is for you to desire to know more of the hope to which he calls you.

*O*pen the eyes of your heart to see the richness that God offers you as his child.

As you go about your business today, pray with a focused kind of intention that the eyes of your heart will be open to all that God has for you. Smile at his generous spirit and his pleasure in giving you all good things.

RENEWED FOR A PURPOSE

Lord, thank you for all that you give me. Help me stay mindful of what I have in you forever and always. I am awed by you. Amen.

Unexpected Company

Happy are those whom he finds alert, even if he comes at midnight or just before dawn. But know this, if the homeowner had known what time the thief was coming, he wouldn't have allowed his home to be broken into.

You also must be ready, because the Human One is coming at a time when you don't expect him.

—Luke 12:38-40

Are you the kind of person whose house is always spotless, always in great shape no matter what?

If so, you probably don't mind the occasional visit by someone you weren't expecting, someone who just dropped by without calling first.

This Scripture is a little daunting because it's suggesting to us that it might be a good idea to get our house in order and keep it that way. After all, we never know when company is coming, and in this case, it could be the King of the Universe.

Are you ready then? Any time now the One who created you is coming back, and he wants you to be ready for him. He wants you to have your affairs in order in a way that shows him how happy you are to see him. He'll be expecting you to anticipate his arrival and to be ready on a moment's notice to offer a warm embrace.

> *K*eep your house in order because you never know when Jesus will drop by.

Might be a good day to take a little inventory of just how ready you are for his visit.

Renewed for a Purpose

Lord, I have to admit that some days, I'm sure I'm ready for you to come and visit and other days, I'm hoping you delay a little. Help me be ready and waiting with open arms for your return. Amen.

What Do You Do for God's People?

*I pray that your partnership in the faith might
become effective by an understanding of all that
is good among us in Christ. I have great joy and encouragement
because of your love, since the hearts
of God's people are refreshed by your actions.*

—Philemon 6-7

Take a few moments and think about the people who make a difference in your life. They may be family members who have helped you through hard times, celebrated with you through great times, or simply lent you a hand when you had a big household project to do. You may think of your church family and the people you see Sunday after Sunday whom you don't know well, but you've come to count on seeing because you all belong there. Who else? Maybe you think of a good friend who has been with you through thick and thin.

These are the people who have given meaning to your life, contributing to you in ways that enrich your days and give you reasons to be happy. These are the people you may well thank God for because of their love and their faithfulness.

> *T*hink of the people who make a difference in your life; make a difference in the life of another.

In the same way, we can lead others to Christ any time we open our hearts in a way that allows a person to get close enough to us to see God's light within us. The more they see of his light, the more they want to know. Shine your light today for all of God's people.

Renewed for a Purpose

Lord, thank you for loving me so much and for reminding me to see every person I meet as one of your children. Help me open my heart in such a way that others see you. Amen.

I Can't Believe You Said That!

Jesus called the crowd near and said to them, "Listen and understand. It's not what goes into the mouth that contaminates a person in God's sight. It's what comes out of the mouth that contaminates the person."

—Matthew 15:10-11

Did you ever hear someone say something that just caught you totally off guard, made you stop everything and wonder that such a thing came out of her or his mouth? We've probably all done it, said things we regret, maybe even wondering why.

It's interesting how careful we are about some things. We wash our hands before we eat dinner. We wash off the vegetables before we cook them after we bring them home from the store. We look at the expiration dates on the stuff in our refrigerators, not wanting to put anything in our mouths that might be contaminated. Then what gives? Why aren't we just as concerned about what comes out of our mouths?

Why don't we scrutinize the things we say that could hurt others and even change their lives forever?

Whether we witness for God directly or our behavior witnesses for God indirectly, we are responsible for the things we say and do. Let us always be

> *T*ake responsibility for what you say, building up and not tearing down those you meet.

aware of what comes out of our mouths that will not benefit others.

RENEWED FOR A PURPOSE

Lord, I'm as guilty as the next person about not always being fully aware of what I say that may be hurtful or unkind. Help me be a witness for you in all the best ways. Amen.

Gaining a New Perspective

Aren't five sparrows sold for two small coins?
Yet not one of them is overlooked by God. Even the hairs
on your head are all counted. Don't be afraid.
You are worth more than many sparrows.

—Luke 12:6-7

The good news for you is that God is in the details. He knows your thoughts, your heart, your hopes, and even the number of hairs on your head. That must mean he's very close to you all the time, since that number most likely changes every few hours. God is near you all the time for only one reason.

He chose you. He values you. He knows that with his help you can do amazing things for his kingdom. He bought you for a great deal more than two small coins. He knows what you're worth.

If all that is true, you need to be in the details too. You need to stay closely connected to your Creator so that you know at any moment what he wants you to do in any situation. Does he want you to lend a hand to a stranger or give a talk to your friends at church? Does he want you to give to a specific charity or pray more? You can only know those things when you're willing to look at the little, even mundane things to see

> *P*ay attention to the details—in doing so you may find opportunity to advance the kingdom.

what they might mean or how you might use them for God's glory.

Remember how much value God puts on the life of each person you meet. Walk right beside him today.

Renewed for a Purpose

Lord, you take care of me so well that I sometimes don't realize how often you've been there in the smallest detail of my life. I praise and thank you for being there every time I need you. Amen.

Risky Business

Send your bread out on the water because, in the course of time,
you may find it again.

—Ecclesiastes 11:1

God must be a risk-taker. After all, he made this universe, saw that everything was good, and then made human beings. He had to have wondered just for a second whether that was one of his better ideas. He took the risk so he could build a relationship with a being who was more akin to himself.

His creative Spirit surely hoped for the best possible outcome, yet, he also knew what would happen since he is God, after all. He knew the whole scene, every being that would be born, every century that would pass, and he knew it would contain people who were absolutely worth the risk. He knew what he was doing when he made you.

Sometimes, you have to cast your bread upon the waters too. You have to put everything you've got out there and hope for the best. You've got to take a chance on life and see if you win. It's the only way to get the reward.

God risked his Son, his heart, and his love. He risked it all for one reason . . . so you could have a home with him one day. That's how much he wanted a

Cast your bread upon the waters: step out in faith as God leads you.

relationship with you. Show him in any way you can that you were definitely worth the risk.

Renewed for a Purpose

Lord, thanks for creating the universe, creating the life I have. Help me be willing to step out in faith for you. Amen.

You're a Piece of Cake!

We know that God works all things together for good
for the ones who love God, for those who are called according to
his purpose. We know this because God knew them in advance,
and he decided in advance that they would be conformed
to the image of his Son.

—Romans 8:28-29

Before you had a resume or a bio that could impress anybody, you were known. God knew all about you in advance. He designed the very purpose for which you were born.

We might think of your relationship with God like a recipe. You know that you'd love to make a homemade chocolate cake. You can see an image of the cake in your mind and taste it from past experience. God didn't picture you as a chocolate cake, but, in the same way, he knew there was a very special recipe that would make you the beautiful person you are. He then prepared all the ingredients. He gave you just the right DNA and just the right family to nurture you for his purposes.

You may not yet be all that he designed you to be, but he knows you have everything it takes to get there. He knows that you were made for an important

> *U*nderstand that God made you the way you are for a purpose, and he thinks you're beautiful.

reason. He knows because he knew you way before you were born. He thinks you're beautiful!

RENEWED FOR A PURPOSE

Lord, I'm not always sure if I have everything it takes to do what you want me to do, but I'm willing to try. I ask that you would reshape me in any way you need to so that I can fulfill my reason for being in this world. Amen.

Laying a Strong Foundation

By wisdom a house is built; by understanding
it is established. By knowledge rooms are filled
with all precious and pleasant wealth.

—Proverbs 24:3-4

When we build something, anything, we need to position it on a strong foundation. Certainly a house needs to be built on land that will support it. A marriage needs to be built on ideals and dreams and realities that will give the couple all they need to grow and strengthen each other. A business can't be built without a good business plan.

We're always building a new house in one sense because the body we live in houses who we are and provides the support we need to live and grow and change. We definitely need wisdom as we create blueprints for the life we hope God will honor and bless. Our greatest assets, then, our building blocks, must start with Jesus, the cornerstone of all that really matters.

As we branch out from there, steadying ourselves through prayer, digging into the Word for a stronger foundation, we're filled with wisdom and knowledge. The more you and I reach out to God to receive his direction, the more he can clear the way for us and help us develop into the beings he meant for us to become.

Build the foundation of your life on Jesus, praying and studying the bible and growing in wisdom.

Only Christ can offer a foundation that is true. Build with wisdom on the rock that can support you forever.

RENEWED FOR A PURPOSE

Lord, thank you for guiding me and helping me grow in knowledge in the work I do. Help me then apply wise choices for the good of others. Amen.

Getting a Good Portion

Give, and it will be given to you. A good portion—
packed down, firmly shaken,
and overflowing—will fall into your lap.

—Luke 6:38

Wouldn't you love a windfall? Maybe a sweet surprise, or some unexpected funds, or some good news from someone you love. If you hope for those things and anticipate them, you actually have a part in causing them to come to fruition. Your part is to ease up on others, stop making judgments about what they should be or what they aren't, and start forgiving.

It would be interesting to keep a running tally of the ways we think about others during the day. Would we be able to balance the score at all with how much we were willing to forgive others or how much we were willing to give to those in need? Would we find that our generosity would surprise even us?

When you tip the scales in the direction of doing good, in the arena of giving whatever you can of your time and money and resources, then there's a promise attached. You'll cause something wonderful to happen. You'll find a windfall suddenly appearing in your lap. God will reward you for your kindness and your generosity. He'll see to it that you receive according to the level at which you give.

> *G*ive generously and God will see and reward you with even more generosity.

RENEWED FOR A PURPOSE

Lord, thank you for giving me the things I have. Thanks for the multitude of blessings you so often send my way. Amen.

Put Your Heart Into It!

Whatever you do, do it from the heart for
the Lord *and not for people. You know*
that you will receive an inheritance as a reward.

—Colossians 3:23-24

Few of us have glamorous jobs or the kind of lives that will end up on reality TV shows. We seldom have more money than we know what to do with, and we're not so destitute that we have to stand on street corners doing a song and dance with our hat in our hands. As believers, though, we might conclude that wherever we are today, we're in exactly the right place. We're in the place God called us to be in for right now. We're his field soldiers, his eyes and ears. More than any of that, though, we're his heart.

Billy Graham once said that "you might be the only Bible some people ever read." What that means, perhaps, is that when someone spends time riding in your car, or calls you with a concern, in need of your friendship and patience, or your skills at any level, they need to see God's heart reflected in you.

Whatever work you have to do today, lift your arms in praise to God and declare that anything you do, you do for him. Your work will seem lighter, and your

> *G*o about your activities today aware that everything you do, you do for God.

heart will feel brighter. May you work with all your heart today.

RENEWED FOR A PURPOSE

Lord, I thank you for the work I get to do each day according to your plan, your design, and your grace. Help me do what pleases you today. Amen.

Energy Boost

*But those who hope in the L*ORD *will renew*
their strength; they will fly up on wings
like eagles; they will run and not be tired;
they will walk and not be weary.

—Isaiah 40:31

Been dragging your heels a bit lately? Wondering where you'll get the moxie to keep doing the things you do when nothing seems to be going in your direction?

It's time to spread your wings! It's time to get out there and put your hope in the Lord. Oh sure, that sounds like what you do all the time, but is it? How often do you really come to him in prayer and surrender your daily walk, surrender your own ego, and look to him to renew your strength?

You may hope in the Lord in small ways or hope timidly. You can take a tiny cup to the ocean and hope God would allow you to fill it up. You can, but why would you? Instead, go to the One who made the ocean and ask to be filled from head to toe, ask for buckets unending of his strength. You're sure to find your wings. It's your day for a great energy boost.

Ask for strength and power like an eagle; ask to run this race in life and not grow weary.

RENEWED FOR A PURPOSE

Lord, thank you for renewing my hope. Help me rise again in joy knowing that you are working all things out for my good. Thank you, Lord, for loving me so much. Amen.

Quiet, Please: Exam in Progress!

Examine yourselves to see if you are in the faith. Test yourselves.
Don't you understand that Jesus Christ is in you?

—2 Corinthians 13:5

If Jesus Christ is inside of you, he is there to help you develop your faith. He wants you to know the Father more fully. He wants you to get to know him too. The idea here is that you may need to test yourself now and then, making sure you're on the path and that your faith is growing. How might you do that today?

One writer said, "God does not require you to follow His leadings on blind trust. Behold the evidence of an invisible intelligence pervading everything, even your own mind and body."

In other words, God hasn't made it difficult for you to determine he is there. He is in everything, the evidence of his presence is in all things, even your body. If that's the case, the test is for you to observe, to feel, and to invite a greater awareness of him into your life. The test of your faith is about desiring even more of what God has to offer you on one hand, and then on the other hand working in

a way that gives him back all that you came here to do. Your faith is in God, not in your work, not in your possibilities, and not in yourself—just in him.

> *Desire to know Jesus more fully—having that desire is a test of your faith.*

RENEWED FOR A PURPOSE

Lord, thank you for being the force that sticks with me even when I forget to listen or act. Help me be faithful in everything I do. Amen.

You're a Shining Star!

Do everything without grumbling and arguing so that you may be blameless and pure, innocent children of God surrounded by people who are crooked and corrupt.
Among these people you shine like stars in the world because you hold on to the word of life.

—Philippians 2:14-16

If you stay still for just a moment and lean in, you might be able to hear it. Can you hear the applause, the ones surrounding you cheering you on because they are so excited you've gotten this far? You've managed against all odds to stay the course in a world where the grumblers and mumblers are abundant; you stand out. You're like a shining star in the middle of a big dark sky.

Sure, you may wonder whether it's all worth it, or whether you want to keep trying. There are days when you could just hide your light under a bushel, but you allow his word to be an actual lamp to your feet, a light to your eyes, and a halo over your head and you keep going.

Oh, there it is again—more cheering, more angels surrounding you, rejoicing with you over the good you've accomplished and the things you've done.

> *L*et your life be a contrast to corrupt people, those who lie and blame others for their misdeeds.

People may tease you a bit about your innocent ways, but more than that, they may wish they could be more like you. Yes, they can all see what a difference it makes. Bravo for you!

RENEWED FOR A PURPOSE

Lord, you keep me steadily on the path of your love, helping me stand even when everything around me feels shaky. You're my rock. Thank you. Amen.

Making a Fool of Yourself!

So be careful to live your life wisely, not foolishly. Take
advantage of every opportunity because these are evil times.

—Ephesians 5:15-16

Someone once said that wise people learn more from the fools in this world than fools learn from those who are wise. So what about you? If this is a two-sided coin, which way do you want the coin to fall? You can choose. You can be wise or foolish on your own.

Your goals and dreams are yours. Some would call them foolish and remind you that you need to take a wiser course of action. Others would call you wise for believing and trusting the God of your heart even when things look improbable, or even impossible.

Jonathan Swift, that fabulous author of Gulliver's Travels, said this: "A person should never be ashamed to own being wrong, for it simply means you are wiser today than you were yesterday." If you need more wisdom today, then start your day with the Source of all knowledge, the one who knows you perfectly.

Embarrassing moments happen to everyone. You can survive a red face and a moment of discomfort, but you'll discover the best wisdom comes when you seek God's Word and his guidance.

Seek God's Word and guidance so that you lead a life filled with wisdom.

RENEWED FOR A PURPOSE

Lord, I am a little crazy sometimes and I'm so glad you hold me up and keep me strong. Help me desire more of your wisdom in every choice I make. Amen.

Giving Your Whole Heart

He replied, "You must love the LORD your God with all your
heart, with all your being, and with all your mind. This is the
first and greatest commandment. And the second is like it: You
must love your neighbor as you love yourself."

—Matthew 22:37-39

Do you ever notice how many things you do with kind of a half-hearted approach? You go to a job that pays you well enough to keep going, but not enough to make you stop wishing you could come up with another plan. You go to Bible study on Tuesdays, but most of the time you feel only partially present because life issues are in the forefront of your mind.

Jesus told us that God wants the whole of us, the whole heart and mind of us. He wants our whole being to love him. That means we have to wake in the morning with him as our first thought, our first love. It means we come to him before we let anything get out of hand. We surrender our days, our relationships, our children, and our jobs to him. We give him thanks and praise for all we have.

Overflowing with that kind of love, we're ready to give more. We can embrace our neighbors and friends, our co-workers and even acquaintances with a love that comes from the heart, from the depth of our being.

> *Give your entire self to Jesus, loving him and your neighbor as much as you love yourself.*

RENEWED FOR A PURPOSE

Lord, I come to you today with my whole heart, surrendering all that I am, all that I can be, and all that I dream about, knowing I'm safe in your love. Amen.

What Time Is It for You?

There's a season for everything and a time
for every matter under the heavens: a time for giving birth
and a time for dying, a time for planting
and a time for uprooting what was planted,
a time for killing and a time for healing, a time for
tearing down and a time for building up.

—Ecclesiastes 3:1-3

Time always wins. Every decade we live influences the way we think about time. When we're young, it seems like forever before we're old enough to have the independence we crave and go on and do the things we dream about. As we move up the scale, time just simply gets shorter until it finally seems to evaporate.

What time is it for you? Is it time to get past a fear that has held you back for years? Is it time for you to get off the sofa and meet the new neighbors down the street or time to remind your spouse how grateful you are to have such a loving relationship? Is it time to renew your connection to God?

We might think that we can keep putting things off until tomorrow, keep waiting for what might be a better time, but the truth is "there is no time like the

> *T*ake time today to express appreciation and love for others, renewing relationships.

present," and in fact, there is no time BUT the present. It's a new day, a new time, a new opportunity for you to make the most of it. You're already on borrowed time!

RENEWED FOR A PURPOSE

Lord, I know I take time for granted. I don't use it wisely and I let it melt away. Then, I find myself rushing everywhere to get things done. Help me invest my time wisely. Amen.

The Right Utensils

Doesn't the potter have the power over the clay
to make one pot for special purposes and another
for garbage from the same lump of clay?

—Romans 9:21

Sometimes we may wonder why God has us working in a certain job or living in a certain town. We feel more like a fish out of water than like a clay pot set in the window for a special reason. We may begin to question our Creator about his plans, even suggesting he may have made a mistake giving us the task at hand.

In our worst state, we might even suggest he didn't do a very good job making us. After all, we're not as smart as some, not as attractive as others. We're not as skilled as our neighbor or as strong as we might be.

The truth is God designed you, and he believes you're some of his best handiwork. He sees you as good and knows what you can do. You have a purpose, and he's excited to see you thrive as you do his work. It's a new day and rather than wonder or question why you

were created, give God thanks and praise for making you exactly as you are, and ask him to guide you into doing all that you can to fulfill your purpose.

> *T*hank God for how you were made, because he made you for his special purposes.

RENEWED FOR A PURPOSE

Lord, I know I don't always understand what you want from me, but I'm grateful to be here. Help me give you the best of me every place I happen to be today. Amen.

A Splash of the Spirit

The Spirit and the bride say, "Come!" Let the one who hears say, "Come!" And let the one who is thirsty come! Let the one who wishes receive life-giving water as a gift.

—Revelation 22:17

The invitations have been sent out. You're invited to come to a fabulous party and it will be overflowing with fountains of joy, refreshing spirits, and reasons to toast the host over and over again. You're invited to a life-giving and life-changing bash and you'll be splashed with the spirit of God. Why were you invited? You asked if you could come. You put your name on the roster the day you accepted the love of Christ. You felt thirsty in your soul and parched in your spirit and you fell in love.

Everything suddenly made sense to you as you learned more of what God's engraved, personal invitation could mean. What refreshment, what joy to be found!

On days when you're parched, living in the desert of the world's traps and confusion, you have a fountain, a place to come to restore your soul. Visit often. Never go thirsty because you have an endless spring of living water ready to keep you strong and nourished.

> *C*ome and restore your soul, remembering those first moments when God opened your eyes.

Come to the waters of God's love today and again tomorrow. He will be there waiting with a cool, refreshing taste of all that is yet to come.

RENEWED FOR A PURPOSE

Lord, thank you for taking care of me even now. Thanks for giving me a place to come and grow and be refreshed in you. Amen.

You Are God's Accomplishment!

*Instead, we are God's accomplishment, created in
Christ Jesus to do good things. God planned for these good things
to be the way that we live our lives.*

—Ephesians 2:10

It always feels good to get something accomplished, to feel like you did something worthwhile and well. That's what God must have experienced when he made you. God gave you a very particular set of skills so that you would be well equipped to accomplish the tasks he put before you.

He allows you to work in the same manner a consultant does in the sense that you can work the plan in a variety of ways, and he'll be pleased with it as long as you get the intended result. In fact, the more creative you are with how you get to the goal, the more enjoyable it can be. The key is simple. You have to keep God informed of your steps.

As long as you go back to God with your game plan and give him a chance to make suggestions and bless it, things will go well, however we often walk off and start doing things without God's blessing.

> *G*o to God so that he can guide and bless you as you accomplish all that is good.

Today you have another opportunity to go back to God and ask him to guide you, offer insights, and bless your work. If you do, then together you'll be able to enjoy some major accomplishments.

RENEWED FOR A PURPOSE

Lord, I know I often make plans and forget to invite you into them. Please see what I'm doing today and help me carry out the mission we have together. Amen.

In the Footprint of Leaders

*Jesus knew the Father had given everything
into his hands and that he had come from God
and was returning to God. So he got up from the table
and took off his robes. Picking up a linen towel,
he tied it around his waist. Then he poured water
into a washbasin and began to wash the disciples' feet,
drying them with the towel he was wearing. When Jesus
came to Simon Peter, Peter said to him,
"LORD, are you going to wash my feet?"*

—John 13:3-6

The idea of servant leadership starts with this Scripture. This is the moment when we see that to lead others, we have to be motivated by our willingness to serve them. We have to set their needs before our own and create opportunities for them to stand firmly on their own two feet.

In serving others, we want not only to be willing to do whatever it takes to get the job done but also to be willing to guide and teach and assist their walk with God in numerous ways. In Bible times, washing the feet of guests was considered a way to honor them because the streets

> *S*erve others as you lead them to a greater understanding of the love Jesus has for them.

were dusty and most people walked a long way in their sandals. You can imagine how inviting it would be to have your feet washed and cleansed and refreshed. Imagine Jesus washing your feet with great love today, preparing you to step out in greater faith to get your work done.

Renewed for a Purpose

Lord, only you can really wash me clean, so I thank you for renewing my spirit in you and staying with me every step of the way. Amen.

Hitting the Jackpot

Generous persons will prosper; those who refresh others will themselves be refreshed.

— Proverbs 11:25

Have you ever considered what you'd do if you won the lottery or somehow managed to win or receive an unexpected but fabulous fortune? After you got over the excitement of the event and paid off your house and all your loans, you might start thinking about giving to others. You might start to imagine how good it would feel to share your good fortune.

The good news is this. You've already won the lottery. You already have a vast fortune to share with others. It may not be showing up in your bank account, but it's there. It's the spirit of generosity that came into your life the day you started following Jesus.

It's the day you said, whatever I have, I'm willing to share. You have been blessed with an abundance of treasure, and the more you give that treasure away, the more blessed you are. C. S. Lewis reminded us that "nothing is really ours until we share it."

It's a new day and the perfect moment to look at what you have to give away. It may just be a moment of your time, a smile, a kind word to the taxi driver, but

> *G*ive something away today: a kind word, extra attention, or a material blessing.

whatever it is, share it. Love is never witnessed by a clenched fist, but only through an open and generous hand.

RENEWED FOR A PURPOSE

Father, you have blessed me beyond measure. You have filled my home and heart with joy. Cause me to never forget what you've done for me and to always remember to give in any way I can to others. Amen.

You Look like Your Father

Instead, renew the thinking in your mind by the Spirit and clothe yourself with the new person created according to God's image in justice and true holiness.

—Ephesians 4:23-24

Most of us take it as a compliment when someone tells us we look like a parent or a favorite relative. We want to reflect the people we love in a positive way. How wonderful when we reflect the likeness of our Father, the God who made us in his own image.

How do we do that? What can we do so that others will see his mannerisms in our walk and talk, see his glow in our faces? One of the keys to changing our image is right here in this verse. It says that we must renew our thinking; we must renew our minds by God's Spirit. When you're excited about life and the way you look, you also have a tendency to dress differently. In fact, you may be motivated to buy a new outfit to reflect the new you. You're more apt to want to look appealing to people in every way because you're happy about the way you look.

It's a great day to clothe yourself in God's image, to wear his smile for all those who see you, and share his heart with each one you meet. Change your

> *R*enew your mind by God's love, reflecting his image by your true and just actions.

thoughts, change your clothes, and create a style all your own . . . one that reflects your love for your Father.

RENEWED FOR A PURPOSE

Lord, I do want to look and act and be more like you. Help me think about you in such a way that I naturally reflect you in the things I do. Help others see your face any time they look at me. Amen.

What's Stopping You?

I assure you that if you have faith the size of a mustard seed, you could say to this mountain, "Go from here to there," and it will go. There will be nothing that you can't do.

—Matthew 17:20

What keeps us from going after the bigger seeds of faith? Why don't we go for apple-seed faith or all the way to watermelon-seed faith? What if we really planted our faith, grounding it in Christ in such a way that nothing could shake us? Maybe then we could grow it into something sizable enough to make the earth move or to influence the direction of a stream.

Jesus could raise people from the dead, stop the winds and waves, and heal the blind. He told his disciples that with the help of the Holy Spirit, they could do greater things than even he had done. Either we're not tapping into the most powerful Source in the universe, or we're walking around with tiny little bits of faith.

If you examine your own faith, perhaps you can identify the things that stop you from wanting more of it. You may be concerned that if you had those powers, God would expect you to use them. You may also be slightly challenged by the idea that your faith should serve not only you,

> *B*e bold enough to practice mustard-seed faith and change the world for good.

but others. Let's learn to practice mustard-seed faith and see what grows from it.

RENEWED FOR A PURPOSE

Lord, you know how much I rely on you and on the faith you've given me. Grant me more faith and a heart that is open to taking it in and sharing it with others. Amen.

Keep Working on Yourself

*Focus on working on your own development
and on what you teach. If you do this, you will save
yourself and those who hear you.*

—1 Timothy 4:16

God wants you to make it your business to develop who and what you are. He wants you to understand your role in being his child and to do what you can to reach and teach others.

Getting to know yourself sounds easy on a superficial level.

You may like the person you try to project to the world. If you dig down a little further, though, you'll come to that layer just under the skin where you hide the things you aren't sure about. That part of you is not as often revealed to others. Then, somewhere buried inside yourself too is the you who truly wants to understand the mysteries of life, the you who wonders about purpose and about God's plans and what part you really are to play in those plans.

God wants you to keep working on yourself, tossing out the stuff that doesn't serve you or him well and looking for the things that resonate with your heart and excite your spirit. The closer you get to that person, the more you'll be able to work for your heavenly Father. He likes the skin you're in,

> *D*ig deep within yourself to find what resonates with your heart and excites your spirit.

but he wants you to get comfortable with the places deep in your heart. You're not thin-skinned or thick-skinned. You're absolutely perfect in God's sight because he has you under his skin.

Renewed for a Purpose

Lord, I'm still learning and there's no doubt about that. Help me develop every aspect of my character in ways that please you. Amen.

The Chameleon in You!

I act weak to the weak, so I can recruit the weak. I have become all things to all people, so I could save some by all possible means. All the things I do are for the sake of the gospel, so I can be a partner with it.

—1 Corinthians 9:22-23

You're pretty adaptable! You change your stripes when you need to. You're comfortable in most settings, whether they're formal or easy-going. You can hike a little, dance a little, and cheer on your favorite baseball team. You've got a little chameleon in you. It's a good thing!

In this letter to the Corinthians, Paul says that is what he tries to do too. He tries to adapt to the situation in the hope that he'll be able to serve or lead, as the need may be, the people who are around him. Jesus was a great example of that for us as well. He met people right where they were and, without judging, shared his heart and his spirit. He gave them what they needed, even if sometimes they weren't really sure what that was.

You have what it takes to become what you need to so that you can relate in very positive and uplifting ways to the people around you. You may not know

> *Be* what you need to be today in order to attract someone to the message of God's love.

what they need. They may not know what they need, but God does. Today be ready to change your direction, your thoughts, and your heart at a moment's notice for the good of someone you meet.

RENEWED FOR A PURPOSE

Lord, you always are there to meet us where we are. You are all things to all people. Help me be more of what you would have me be in any situation I face today. Amen.

Another Shot of Caffeine!

Stay awake, stand firm in your faith, be brave, be strong.
Everything should be done in love.

—1 Corinthians 16:13-14

Some mornings, no matter how much coffee you pour into your veins, you can't quite wake up. It's like you're in a sleep hangover and no matter what you do, you're just slightly off center. You're somewhere between that sleepy dream state and that wakeful, jump-back-into-the-world state.

No amount of caffeine will be able to wake you up enough to get your spirit's motor running. Only God can do that. He does it through turning up the light of your faith. It's through faith that he can strengthen you, firm up your direction and your resolve to get you going again.

Faith then is the thing you have to drink in and feed upon. It alone can starve your doubts.

As you wake up to the people God has put into your life, all for his great purpose, be sure to meet them with joy and with love. So remember today that God is not looking for you to seek him with your mind and your feelings, things that a little caffeine may help you with. He's looking for you to experience him today through faith and love.

> *W*ake up to God's great purpose and greet the people you meet today with joy and love and gratitude.

RENEWED FOR A PURPOSE

Lord, I know I'm not always awake to the things you have for me, the love you give me and the mercy you offer me. Grant me the faith and the love to see those things in you and share them with those around me. Amen.

And God Saw That It Was Good!

*Let's not get tired of doing good, because in time we'll
have a harvest if we don't give up. So then, let's work for the good
of all whenever we have an opportunity,
and especially for those in the household of faith.*

—Galatians 6:9-10

When God was busy creating the world we know, he looked at each step he took and was pleased. He thought it was good. He looked forward to what the world would be like given the amount of goodness he put into it. Because all goodness can only be measured against his standards, we sometimes weary of doing good. We sometimes wonder if the good we do matters at all or if it even makes a difference.

God sees your work and your good intent. He sees your heart and what motivates you to do good things, and it pleases him.

Meister Eckhart said, "Do what good you can, and do it solely for God's glory, as free from it yourself as though you did not exist. Ask nothing whatever in return. Done in this way, your works are spiritual and godly."

> Do not grow weary of doing good because it does make a difference in the long run.

The world needs more good. We're somewhat off kilter, out of balance, and hungry for the things that bring truth and meaning to life. We need to see goodness as the beautiful thing it was meant to be. We need to do all the good we can for as many people as possible.

RENEWED FOR A PURPOSE

Lord, thank you for giving me opportunities to do good. Help me be more generous every day with all the gifts you've given me. Amen.

Complete in Love

If you love only those who love you, what reward
do you have? Don't even the tax collectors do the same?
And if you greet only your brothers and sisters,
what more are you doing? Don't even the Gentiles do
the same? Therefore, just as your heavenly
Father is complete in showing love
to everyone, so also you must be complete.

—Matthew 5:46-48

Matthew reminds us that love isn't just about the people we're comfortable with, or the people who make us happy, or the people we relate to in some special way. Love is about our neighbors. It's about people we haven't met and never will. It's about doing what we can in the name of love for humankind. That's complete love, not excluding anyone simply because we don't have a personal kinship with them.

The ancient philosopher Tertullian said, "It is our care for the helpless, our practice of loving kindness, that brands us in the eyes of many of our opponents." He continues, "'Look! . . . How they love one another."

Love not only your family but also those who may not at first appear to be lovable.

Love is an action word, and it is our mission to become better lovers, better givers, and better caretakers of others. That is what completes us. Reach out in love today.

RENEWED FOR A PURPOSE

Father, I am a neophyte in the arena of love. I love those who are near me, but I often neglect to seek out and embrace those outside my personal circle of friends. Help me be willing to love one more person today. Amen.

Here's Your Promotion!

His master replied, "Excellent! You are a good and faithful servant! You've been faithful over a little. I'll put you in charge of much. Come, celebrate with me."

—Matthew 25:21

Most of us won't get an Academy Award for our performance in this life. We may not even be up for the Best Supporting Actor. We're most likely the ones who are always behind the scenes, doing the little things to try to make a difference. We serve others to help make their names greater, whether we serve our bosses or our families or someone else who has a specific calling.

We serve God to make his name greater, too. We are good and faithful servants when we willingly do the tasks God has asked of us. We may not think he notices our efforts or that anyone else does for that matter. We don't do it to win any awards. The truth is that God sees us and sees our work all the time.

Whatever role he has given us is never too small to be of service to him. Now and then, he calls us out of that job and promotes us to a new position. That's his way of rewarding us, promoting us and putting us over even more of his projects. God needs you to play the role he's given you, and he will

> *S*erve God wherever he puts you because it's important, whether you're lead actor or camera crew.

raise you up in his own time. He loves what you do as his good and faithful servant.

RENEWED FOR A PURPOSE

Lord, I don't know if my small contributions make a kingdom difference or not, but I trust you'll let me know if you want me to do something else. Thanks for being with me today. Amen.

You're Such a Gift!

Serve each other according to the gift each person has received,
as good managers of God's diverse gifts.

—1 Peter 4:10

A gift is a wonderful thing. It is pleasant to receive, more wonderful to give, and it is in the spirit of giving that we come to serve each other. Unlike the packaged variety, our gifts can't be used up, don't need to be dusted, and aren't likely to spoil. We have gifts that are God-given, and they last forever.

Our individual and collective gifts are meant to be a contribution to help others live better and happier lives. We can use our writing talents to share stories of God's love, to offer insights and perspective that may be new, to make someone laugh. We can use our analytical gifts to help someone organize, prioritize, and balance laws of science, money, and investments. We can use our creative talents in every way under the sun, and we can teach and preach and reach people with our hope and our optimism and our gifts of the Spirit.

In other words, we have no excuse; we each have gifts and those gifts are needed for the good of others. We are meant to use our gifts in any way we can

> *U*se your God-given gifts—yes, you have them—to contribute to the well-being of others.

for our good and the good of those we meet along the way.

RENEWED FOR A PURPOSE

Lord, remind me today that I have been given great gifts that I can use for your glory to help others in your name. Amen.

You're So Brave!

But we aren't the sort of people who timidly draw back and end up being destroyed. We're the sort of people who have faith so that our whole beings are preserved.

—Hebrews 10:39

Faith gets the credit for doing a lot of things. It gets you through the weird things, the tough times, the craziness that life can bring. It gives you reasons to keep hoping for the good things and challenges you when you're somewhat dismayed. It's your friend, your confidante, your strength partner. Faith is the living, breathing essence of what makes you a believer. It's your lifeline!

It's not always easy to put faith ahead of fear, but it's possible. God has given you a way to get past those things that strike fear into your heart. The closer you get to him, the more he can do. The greater your weakness, the more he sends in the cavalry, marshalling the troops to give you whatever you need to keep going. When fear tempts you to run, run toward the One who has the ability to help you get through any obstacle, who loves you just as you are and works to put all things together for your good.

> *L*et your faith overcome your fears and anxieties because God walks with you.

God thinks you're brave. He sees you coming from miles away, knowing exactly what you need, and he runs toward you with lightning speed. That's what his love does. Nothing can be greater than that!

RENEWED FOR A PURPOSE

Lord, thank you for taking care of me when I'm fearful. I come to you and lean in so I can hear your voice strengthening me and helping me bravely go forward. Amen.

Come Into the Light

Hence, I will also appoint you as light to the nations so that my salvation may reach to the end of the earth.

—Isaiah 49:6

One frequent theme of the Bible is the effect of light and what it does to illuminate truth. God spoke the light into being, making it possible for us to see his world in the backdrop of the darkness. He made it possible for us to see him and to feel the light of his face upon us. Light then serves as an intentional metaphor for guidance and the gift of his presence.

So what happens when we slip into the shadows? Sometimes we step aside from the path, take the lead away from God and walk alone. We stubbornly hold independence as a valuable asset, perhaps the best asset we have. It is valuable, but it isn't everything, especially when we cease to be dependent on God, our source of light. We can only shine for him as we stand in his presence.

You've been given the flame. You are the light. In fact, you may be the only light of God's love that some people will ever see. Your work on this planet is to shine and to help others come into God's presence for themselves.

> *S*tay in God's light so that you may reflect his truth and mercy and forgiveness.

It's a great day to turn on your high beams.

RENEWED FOR A PURPOSE

Lord, I know that I sometimes hide the light you've given me. Help me shine in ways that please you and help others see you in a new way. Amen.

Testing . . . 1, 2, 3!

All the ways of people are pure in their eyes,
but the LORD tests the motives. Commit your work
to the LORD, and your plans will succeed.

—Proverbs 16:2-3

When you set out to accomplish something new, do you ask yourself the questions, "Why am I doing this, and who am I doing it for?"

Most of us have a lot of sound reasons for the things we do. We are motivated by a desire to get ahead, to create more opportunities for ourselves and those around us. We're motivated by a passion for our work or a commitment to our families.

Proverbs 16 reminds us that commitment to ourselves and our families is important, but it's the commitment we make to the Lord that will offer us the biggest chance for success. Committing to him first makes great sense. After all, we want to do his work effectively and well, and we want to make a difference.

You're right to make plans, and you're right to go after fresh opportunities and promotions and those other things that build a fruitful foundation for your family, but you have to check in now and then, actually daily, with the Lord. You have to commit your work to him so that

> *C*ommit your work to God, asking always for his guidance and approval that you may succeed.

your motivations are pure and sound. God wants you to succeed. He wants your work to be blessed. He gave you the gifts you have to accomplish great things.

RENEWED FOR A PURPOSE

Lord, I'm off and running again, but before I go, remind me that I am working for you first and foremost. Inspire me and keep me motivated in ways that are healthy and that will serve you and my family well. Amen.

Like a Watered Garden

The Lord will guide you continually and provide for you, even in parched places. He will rescue your bones. You will be like a watered garden, like a spring of water that won't run dry.

—Isaiah 58:11

Have you ever been really thirsty? You know the kind of thirst that chugging a big glass of water or slamming down a soda just won't cure? It's easy to take getting a glass of water to quench our thirst for granted, even though much of the world struggles to find good drinking water. Many people are thirsty. Many people are parched. Yet even in those places, God offers to be a spring of water that won't run dry.

He parted the waters of the Red Sea and brought his children safely across to dry land. He guided every step and refreshed their spirits with manna and birds. He opened up veins of water from solid rocks to relieve their thirst. God continues to guide and to refresh us wherever we are. He still offers to be our living water if we reach out to him.

If you're feeling a little dry today, needing a bigger splash of his love, then take your little cup and put it out to him. He'll fill it, and then he'll keep filling every

*A*ccept the refreshment offered by the Word and Spirit of God and refresh others.

cup you are willing to put in his hand. Go and get refreshed and renewed in his love today.

RENEWED FOR A PURPOSE

Lord, I am thirsty. Sometimes I don't even realize that I've gotten away from you, but when I do, I know I want to leave the desert I've put myself in and draw from your wellspring of living waters. Renew my heart and my life in you today. Amen.

Gracious Hospitality!

Keep loving each other like family. Don't neglect to open up your homes to guests, because by doing this some have been hosts to angels without knowing it.

—Hebrews 13:1-2

Nobody has the gift for putting a home together like you do! You always know exactly the right touch to make every little nook and cranny more inviting and more homey. You have a style all your own, and it's one of the things God loves so much about you.

In Bible times, there weren't hotels on every other corner, just people who would put travelers up in their homes and catch up on the news. It was usually a good experience for the travelers and for the hosts as well.

Today, we still may be asked to house exchange students who visit our communities from other towns and other countries or missionaries as they pass through the area on a fund-raising tour.

Whatever the opportunity is to invite others into our homes, the idea is to treat them like family. In fact, we're to love them like family.

If we think about it, we're all travelers here on planet earth. We're all here at the invitation of our Creator, and we're just passing through. Today, let's

> *S*hare your hospitality with people who cross your path, treating them as part of God's family.

remember that every person we meet is God's child, and since we have the same Father, we're all family! Who knows, one of them just may be an angel!

RENEWED FOR A PURPOSE

Lord, you have given me so much and I am truly grateful. Help me open my heart to others and embrace each one I meet as family. Amen.

Harvesting the Good Stuff

But the fruit of the Spirit is love, joy, peace, patience, kindness, goodness, faithfulness, gentleness, and self-control. There is no law against things like this.

—Galatians 5:22-23

Imagine a fruit of the Spirit market, much like a farmer's market, where you could go amid the throngs of people and find a rich assortment of love in one booth, a soothing waterfall of peace and patience in another, and some tender sprouts of goodness and kindness just ready to blossom. You're invited into this kind of market every day and the fees are very reasonable. In fact, when you choose the Savior of the world to be your very own, he gives you this bounty as part of the deal.

Oh, you may find yourself shying away from some of the vendors. You may not want to have total self-control, for instance, having to be totally responsible for all your actions, because then it would be hard to pull out those old excuses that have carried you for so long. The truth is you no longer need the old excuses. You've already been excused from all the things that held you back and didn't allow you to bloom. Your life is meant to be fruitful. It's time to reap the harvest!

> *C*laim what God has given you: love, joy, peace, patience, kindness, goodness, faithfulness, gentleness, self control.

God saved all the good stuff just for you. Enjoy!

RENEWED FOR A PURPOSE

Lord, thank you for your incredible gifts to me. Help me receive them and utilize them for the good of others today. Amen.

Stand Firm . . . Take a Bow!

You must stand firm, unshakable, excelling in the work of the LORD as always, because you know that your labor isn't going to be for nothing in the LORD.

—1 Corinthians 15:58

You've probably done a few thankless jobs in your life. You know, those are the jobs where you trudge to work every day, do what you must with as much energy as you can manage, and trudge home again wondering why you keep doing it.

Paul, in his letter to the Corinthians, tells us that when you see what you do as doing work for the Lord, you have every reason to celebrate. His Spirit will supply all the energy you need, and your heart will be light because of the joy you experience.

God has every desire and intention for you to be happy in your work. If you find yourself in the slow lane, trudging your way, begrudging your day, then it might be time for a change. Ask God to help you know whether he wants you in the job you're in. If you're working for him, there will always be a reward. In fact, your future is guaranteed and the benefits are awesome.

Remember the work you do daily is really work you do for the Lord, and it is not without purpose.

RENEWED FOR A PURPOSE

Lord, I know that I don't always feel sure I'm doing the right work. I know I don't give all that I can when my heart isn't in the flow of things. Help me see your hand in the work I do and shine your light so others can see your good works and rejoice. Amen.

How Can I Serve You?

You were called to freedom, brothers and sisters; only don't let
this freedom be an opportunity to indulge your selfish impulses,
but serve each other through love.

—Galatians 5:13

When we walk into a restaurant, we expect the waiters to be enthusiastic about our arrival, pleased to take our order, happy to get us anything we ask for, and thrilled to get our tip at the end of the meal, and then send us on our way smiling.

What if we took it upon ourselves to spend our days treating each other in a similar fashion? We would be creating an opportunity for doors to open through this encounter. We would do this because we are free to offer others a hand as we choose. And we can't help getting something back from our kind deeds because we'll have a genuine sense of satisfaction that we might have made a difference.

Imagine today that you can brighten someone's day just because you showed up. That's your calling. That's the reason you've been gifted with all you are and all you have. That's how you give back to God a small piece of all he has given you. It's your day to cheer up a few more people. Enjoy it!

> *F*ind time to serve others, to make their day, because you shared a kindness, something they needed.

RENEWED FOR A PURPOSE

Lord, thank you for giving me an attitude of graciousness and a spirit of love. Help me serve others as you would have me do. Amen.

Living in Grace

Therefore, once you have your minds ready for action and you
are thinking clearly, place your hope completely on the grace that
will be brought to you when Jesus Christ is revealed.

—1 Peter 1:13

Dietrich Bonhoeffer wrote, "Cheap grace is grace without discipleship, grace without the cross, grace without Jesus Christ, living and incarnate. Costly grace is the treasure hidden in the field; for the sake of it a man will gladly go and sell all that he has."

Most of us appreciate the sense that we live in God's grace. We like knowing we can fall down and get up again without a big penalty. We like knowing God takes us back again after we make a mess of the life he's given us.

We're living right now in his incredible grace. We walk in it, drink it in, and where we can, we direct it toward others. We extend the hand of grace to friends and complete strangers.

This is the kind of action God wants us to take because of the hope he has placed within us. Our hearts and minds are poised and ready to be his voices, his hands, and his tireless feet. We have the treasure of seeing God in everything, of realizing that his hand alone brought all that we have into fruition.

> *B*e gracious today to yourself and those you meet along the way.

Renewed for a Purpose

Lord, I am humbled by your grace, by your forgiveness, and your tenderness toward me. Help me share those very same gifts with everyone around me. Amen.

What You Say Matters

I tell you that people will have to answer on Judgment Day for every useless word they speak. By your words you will be either judged innocent or condemned as guilty.

—Matthew 12:36-37

This has to be one of the scariest Scriptures in the Bible. After all, most of us do a lot of talking. This verse is a good reminder of the benefits of being brief and holding our tongues when the need arises.

What causes us to go on and on when we would be better served to remain silent? Jesus gave us an example of effective silence and limited commentary when he was in front of Pilate being accused of things that simply weren't true.

Many of us have a tendency to either overexplain or demand detailed explanations from someone else, and before we know it, anger erupts and caution is thrown to the wind. We spew things out of our mouths, and if we were to rewind the tape later and listen, we would wince.

Our lesson then is to be very aware of what we say. As we lean in on the Lord, we will have the grace and the kindness to treat others with respect and love. Words like that bless everyone, and apparently even bring blessing back to us.

Be a blessing to others with your smile and kind words today.

Let's be kind today.

RENEWED FOR A PURPOSE

Lord, help me remember that what I say to anyone is important. Let me speak only with forethought, with kindness, and with love. Amen.

Heroes Reluctant and Otherwise

Offer yourself as a role model of good actions. Show integrity, seriousness, and a sound message that is above criticism when you teach, so that any opponent will be ashamed because they won't find anything bad to say about us.

—Titus 2:7-8

You may not think of yourself as a superhero. In fact, when it comes to rescuing others you may be more of a reluctant bystander. The truth is that you're in the spotlight sometimes whether you want to be or not. You are someone else's only example of what it means to be a believer. You're the one they are trying to emulate.

If others are trying to follow your example, then you have to work doubly hard to follow the example of Christ. You have to watch him closely, listen to his voice, and follow him everywhere. If a good example is the best sermon, you might want to be aware of where you are when you flash your cape and enter the room ready to save the lost and the broken-hearted. God knows why he sent you into the midst of the people you work with or the people you bowl with on Sunday nights.

You're God's example, his hero to the people he wants to bring into the kingdom. He chose you to get the job done and all

> *P*reach without words; preach with actions, imitating the love that Jesus has shown you.

you have to do is be a good example of his love.

RENEWED FOR A PURPOSE

Lord, thank you for being my role model, for giving me the divine examples that keep me safe in God's hands. Help me be a better example of your love to those around me. Amen.

Setting Priorities . . . Again!

Instead, desire first and foremost God's kingdom and God's righteousness, and all these things will be given to you as well.

—Matthew 6:33

As you start a new day, take time to look at your priorities, to examine more closely where you are willing to put your effort and energy. What's at the top of your to-do list?

Most likely, you'll find a lot of things there like working hard for that next promotion, studying to get through a course at school, or exercising to get your weight under control. At different times throughout the year, we become pretty focused on improving ourselves and our lot in life.

Matthew recommends that we go back to our to-do list to see if we've remembered to put God at the top of it. He says that when we start there, we're getting it right. In fact, we're getting the message that there's really nothing worth doing if God is not a part of the equation.

Today, put your grocery list aside for a bit and scratch out the stuff that keeps you busy and look for the stuff that keeps you in the business of life, the life God called you to. He can only help you, guide you, and bless you if you invite him into your story. Call him, he's always available to you.

*F*ocus on God's kingdom and his purpose, and in return God will give you an abundant life.

RENEWED FOR A PURPOSE

Lord, I know that I get so busy with life I forget to even mention your name in passing. I forget that you are the reason I get to do anything at all. Be with me today and lead the way to all that you would have me do. Amen.

What Does Your Heart Say?

God doesn't look at things like humans do. Humans see only
what is visible to the eyes, but the LORD sees into the heart.

—1 Samuel 16:7

What if we only saw each other as human beings doing our best to make our way in the world? What if we truly saw each other from the perspective of our heart's view? If we did that, we'd be a lot closer to following the example of Jesus. We'd be more open to meeting people where they are in their walk of faith or their search for meaning. We could let go of doubt and misguided judgments. We could stop searching for hidden motivations.

We could simply let people breathe and live and be all they were meant to be. We could give them what we want for ourselves. We'd be on the cusp of understanding what real love is all about.

Do an experiment today. Make it your intention to look past the way someone is dressed, or the way someone pronounces or mispronounces their words. Look beyond the fact that someone isn't necessarily attractive in your usual terms, and look inside yourself.

Look within yourself and see what your heart knows that you have yet to discover. At the end of the day, think about the people you met and pray for them. Ask

> *L*ook past the outward appearances of people you meet today and understand your commonality.

God to open your heart even more for the day after this one. Look to the eyes of your heart and see if you can make a difference.

RENEWED FOR A PURPOSE

Lord, thank you for not seeing us the way we often see one another. Remind me that I need to do more looking with my heart when it comes to being a better friend and a better servant. Amen.

Believing Is Seeing

By faith Enoch was taken up so that he didn't see death, and he wasn't found because God took him up. He was given approval for having pleased God before he was taken up.

It's impossible to please God without faith because the one who draws near to God must believe that he exists and that he rewards people who try to find him.

—Hebrews 11:5-6

Many of us approach God with a kind of "seeing is believing" mentality, whereas God has more of a "believing is seeing" mentality. The more you believe, the more you'll see. The more you see, the more God draws near to you and is able to approve your plans and dreams.

How can you practice believing? God must know that you believe in him, have complete faith in him, and are totally connected to him regardless of what you see or don't see. God must be a witness to your faith. When he is, then he can reward you and approve your future plans and dreams. To help you practice believing, try this simple exercise and repeat it until you have truly taken it in as your own idea.

> *A*dopt the mentality that believing is seeing, pleasing God who will draw ever nearer.

Say to yourself, "Lord, I totally believe in you and in your love for me. I believe that you are ready to approve my hopes and dreams. Thank you for loving me so much. Amen."

RENEWED FOR A PURPOSE

Lord, I'm faithful most of the time, but I admit I don't always have the assurance I wish I had. I know that sometimes I want you to give me signs of your presence so I know I'm right. Lord, just help me believe more fully in you today. Amen.

Facing the Place of Grace

May you have more and more grace and peace through the knowledge of God and Jesus our LORD.

—2 Peter 1:2

God's got you covered. He's got your back. He bought the added insurance and the protection plan that will bring you back to him as the future unfolds. You live every day under his grace.

Though grace may seem like a simple concept, it's not easy for us to always grasp the gift it truly is and to thank God for it. Abraham Lincoln wrote: "We have forgotten the gracious hand which has preserved us in peace and multiplied and enriched and strengthened us, and have vainly imagined in the deceitfulness of our hearts that all these blessings were produced by some superior wisdom and virtue of our own. Intoxicated with unbroken success, we have become too self-sufficient to feel the necessity of redeeming and preserving grace, too proud to pray to the God that made us."

We are nothing without the love and protection of our Creator and Redeemer. Our job is to call on his name, thank him for all he gives us, and serve him so that others may recognize him and call on him as well. Go in mercy and peace and serve your heavenly Father.

> *R*ecognize that your success comes by the grace of God, and not your own doing.

Renewed for a Purpose

Lord, you have blessed us so abundantly we hardly realize all you've done. Give us grateful hearts to live well according to your grace and mercy. Amen.

Name Droppers

A good name is better than fine oil, and the
day of death better than the birthday.

—Ecclesiastes 7:1

Some people just love to establish their own importance by dropping the names of celebrities or people of influence. They love knowing the head chef at a great restaurant or the mayor of their city. It reflects well on them to have connections with people in high places. What about you?

You certainly know some people in high places. There can't be a higher name throughout heaven and earth than the name of Jesus Christ. He doesn't mind if you become a name dropper on his behalf.

As you reflect on the beauty and the value that comes from the name of Jesus, consider your own name. How might you build it in a way that it brings joy to others and is received as honey and sweetness? The day you were born brought a moment of celebration in the heavens and the day you return will bring even greater joy for the journey you have been on.

Consider your name today and what it means to those around you. Think even more about what it means to you and to your family and friends.

> *B*ring honor to your name by building up others, offering help, and sharing God's grace.

Your name is an honorable one, and it deserves to be respected and protected.

RENEWED FOR A PURPOSE

Lord, thank you for giving me a name that brings honor to me and to my family. Remind me that it is a gift worthy of respect and protection. Bless my family name today and always. Amen.

God's Co-workers

Each one had a role given to them by the Lord:
I planted, Apollos watered, but God made it grow.
Because of this, neither the one who plants nor the one
who waters is anything, but the only one who is
anything is God who makes it grow.

—1 Corinthians 3:5-7

Thinking about your co-workers at the office or those who are part of your fellowship team is one thing. Thinking about having God sitting next to you, just down the aisle, one cubicle over, is another.

The truth is, that's a good picture to keep in mind. You are meant to be part of God's team, working with him to accomplish his mission on earth. In fact, that's your main job. It's the one he brought you here to do.

In his love and mercy, he allows us to shine. Sometimes he lets us lead others right to him. Sometimes he lets us influence the lives of others so that they are changed in ways that please him. Whether we're a televangelist causing more than twenty million viewers to come to Christ or a church youth worker bringing one young teen into the fold, we're still nothing more than part of the team. We were given the opportunity to

> *R*emember you're part of a team that doesn't let players sit on the bench.

plant the seed or refresh the spirit of someone else, but only God has the role of opening the heart in such a way that the seed takes root and the spirit grows in faith. We each have a job to do.

Remember, in all that you do today, God is cheering you on.

RENEWED FOR A PURPOSE

Lord, I know that sometimes I get in there and make things happen by your love and mercy. Help me create those moments today when someone else might see you more clearly. Amen.

Busy as a Bee

As a result of all this, my loved brothers and sisters,
you must stand firm, unshakable, excelling in the work
of the Lord as always, because you know that your labor
isn't going to be for nothing in the Lord.

—1 Corinthians 15:58

Did you ever watch honeybees as they buzz from flower to flower, focused on drinking their fill of glorious nectar, designed to help them produce sweet, succulent, golden rich honey? Interestingly, a single bee only creates about one twelfth of a teaspoon of honey in its lifetime. The bee is very purposeful, though, and never stops trying to get the job done.

How we approach our work, our attitude toward what we do, makes a huge difference in what we're able to accomplish. More than that, it makes a huge difference in how we perceive the importance of our role to get the job done. Whether you're a street cleaner or a school teacher, your work makes a difference. There are fellow workers out there that totally depends on what you do. When you adopt an attitude of joy about your work, you make the angels smile because you show without a doubt that you are doing your work for the Lord.

> *A*pproach your work with joy, knowing that together with other believers you make a difference.

Hope you're busy as a bee today.

RENEWED FOR A PURPOSE

Lord, I am happy to do the work I do, knowing that it pleases you and that you bless the work of my hands with your grace and mercy. Amen.

Love Says, "I'm Sorry!"

Above all, show sincere love to each other, because love brings about the forgiveness of many sins.

— 1 Peter 4:8

Love is a multifaceted thing and one of its best attributes is that it allows us to forgive each other when we mess up. Imagine if you got a scratch on your hand, then you got a bruise on your ankle, and then a scrape on your knee.

Now imagine what you'd look like in a pretty short order if those bruises and scratches didn't heal. What if you had to walk around wearing every one of those bruises for the rest of your life?

Fortunately, God designed us so that we can fall down, get a few scrapes, dust ourselves off, and walk on again. In a pretty short time we'll be healed and good as new.

The same opportunity is yours when it comes to healing the bumps and bruises in your relationships. The people you love sometimes cause you to feel a bit bruised. Sometimes they cut you to the quick, and you feel like even a bandage won't fix it. The truth is, love can fix it. Love is the one thing that can make everything that goes haywire okay again. Love means you know just when to say "I'm sorry" and just when to receive an apology from someone else.

Set a damaged relationship right today by giving or accepting apologies for past hurts.

It's a new day and a new opportunity to heal a bruise and make things whole again with someone you love.

RENEWED FOR A PURPOSE

Lord, I thank you that you love me so much you forgive me over and over again. Remind me often to do the same for others and to remember that it's good to say, "I'm sorry." Amen.

Love . . . There's No Faking It!

Love should be shown without pretending. Hate evil,
and hold on to what is good.

—Romans 12:9

No matter how we address the idea of love, one thing remains true, you simply can't pretend to love something you don't. Sure, you can try it on, test it out, and see if it happens, but eventually you'll set it aside because it simply wasn't genuine. It simply wasn't the real thing.

Of course, great imitations are out there, those experiences that seem real or pass as love for a time, but then can't sustain and so fade away. As a way to gauge this for yourself, put God into the equation. What if his love wasn't genuine? What if he was only pretending to love you? Where would you be?

God can never be anything but genuine and real. He is love. He can only be love. We fall far short of that mark, but he loves us anyway. He says to keep trying. Keep following my example and I'll help you get a sense, a better idea of what real love is all about. He has provided us with amazing examples.

Mother Teresa said this about love: "Spread love everywhere you go: First of all in your own house . . . let no one ever come to you without leaving

Be genuine in your love for others, bringing them joy, by letting God's love shine through you.

better and happier." You can't fake that kind of love. Share the authentic, genuine, unmistakable love in your heart and make it real in all your relationships.

RENEWED FOR A PURPOSE

Lord, you are such a great teacher. Teach me to love fully and completely, genuinely and joyfully for your sake and the sake of others. Let me spread love every place I go today. Amen.

What's Your Reality?

Faith is the reality of what we hope for, the proof of what we don't see.

—Hebrews 11:1

Reality TV is a funny concept. It invites us into a personal encounter with someone we've never met, and before long, we're in a virtual relationship. We think we're part of their lives, and they are part of ours. The problem is that we don't truly know each the other, and chances are good you never will. It's simply not reality.

Sometimes we want faith to be a bit like a reality TV spot. We want to plug in and connect with it, and ultimately make the right choice and come out with the happy ending. We want it to be easy.

The writer of Hebrews reminds us that faith is about a reality we hope for, an outcome we believe in and act on even when we don't have proof. It's a lot like love or appreciation of the arts. No one else can really understand your choices or how you feel, but it's your reality.

Look at the things you have faith in. Furthermore, look at the things you don't have faith in, and check in with your Creator. He is the only reality. He is the proof of what you don't see. Have faith in him and faith in yourself and the things you hope for will begin to come to you according to his will and purpose.

> *O*pen your heart so that greater faith can flow through you to others.

RENEWED FOR A PURPOSE

Lord, I thank you for the gift of faith. Sometimes I have a lot, and I feel on fire for you. Other times, I have a little, and I look to things in this world to give me answers and direction. Help me see all that you want for me with eyes of faith. Amen.

Keep Your Heart Pumping!

May the love cause your hearts to be strengthened, to be blameless in holiness before our God and Father when our LORD Jesus comes with all his people. Amen.

—1 Thessalonians 3:13

We talk about how to keep our hearts healthy, at least in the physical sense. We recognize the sadness of heart disease as it destroys people's lives. As true as it is in our physical nature, it's also true in the spiritual sense. What are we doing to avoid spiritual heart disease? What are we doing to strengthen our hearts on a daily basis?

The heart muscle pumps as long as it can no matter how we take care of it. The problem comes in when we neglect it for too long, when we eat all the wrong things and never exercise, or when we act as though what we do has no consequence. The truth is what we do matters, especially in matters of the heart.

That heart-thumping evangelist Jonathan Edwards said this: "See that your chief study be about your heart: that there God's image may be planted; that there His interests be advanced . . . that there the love of holiness grows."

> *P*lant God's image in your heart so that you can grow in your love of him, advancing his plans.

The heart has a big job to do. Today and every day, check in with your spirit and make sure your heart is being nourished. Ask God to keep your heart and your mind in Christ Jesus. That way, you'll always have a healthy heart.

Renewed for a Purpose

Whatever else I do today, Lord, help me be aware of my heart. Protect it, shape it, and strengthen it according to your will and purpose. I thank you for loving me so much. Amen.

God Works within Us

Glory to God, who is able to do far beyond all that we could ask or imagine by his power at work within us.

—Ephesians 3:20

We were born to do the work God called us to do. Sometimes, we aren't sure what the work is. Sometimes we are afraid to check in with God about our work for fear that the assignment will be too hard or perhaps seem too easy.

We think about the way we work for God with the same energy we think about the work we do at the office, or the work we do at home. With God, the definition may be slightly different, though.

Look at what George McDonald shared about this idea. "Do you think the work God gives us to do is never easy? Jesus says His yoke is easy, His burden light. People sometimes refuse to do God's work just because it is easy. This is sometimes because they cannot believe that easy work is His work."

In other words, don't assume that you aren't doing God's work simply because you're not building houses for Habitat for Humanity or teaching in a mission field. Your ministry may well be to offer hope and encouragement to one special person in your family or in your church. Your work may be to keep pointing the way to God in gentle and affirming ways.

Today, listen for his voice and respond, doing his work with great joy.

RENEWED FOR A PURPOSE

Lord, I don't always hear you speaking. I don't always listen. Today, help me work with you to bless the life of at least one other person. Amen.

You Get by with a Little Help from Your Friends

So continue encouraging each other and building each other up,
just like you are doing already.

—1 Thessalonians 5:11

Look at the headlines of the daily paper in the morning and you may feel the weight of the world on your shoulders. Everywhere you look there is one disaster after another.

You read about tornados raging through small towns and leaving a path of desolation, teenagers going on a killing spree just for fun, children separated from parents, or homeless people needing shelter in zero-degree weather. The list goes on and on, and the heartbreak is endless.

So what is your job? You can't save the world. God already made provisions for that. What you can do, though, is offer help in the form of encouraging words or volunteering some time. You can make a difference right where you live, right where you are.

Make it your goal to be an angel to someone today and offer him or her an encouraging word or a cheerful smile.

> *To someone who is hurting, offer a little light that only you know how to give.*

RENEWED FOR A PURPOSE

Lord, the world seems so heavy, so dark sometimes that it's hard to take in the pain reflected in every news broadcast and daily headline. There's too much CNN and not enough TLC. Help me remember to offer whatever encouragement I can in the things I do today. Amen.

In the Heat of the Battle

I know that good doesn't live in me—that is, in my body.
The desire to do good is inside of me, but I can't do it.
I don't do the good that I want to do, but I do the evil that
I don't want to do. But if I do the very thing that I don't want to
do, then I'm not the one doing it anymore. Instead,
it is sin that lives in me that is doing it.

—Romans 7:18-20

You may not think of it this way, but you're in a constant struggle, a tug of war between the you that wants to do things that will please God enormously and the you that will disappoint God. You want to do the right thing, and God knows you try. He's pulling for you and trying to help any way he can.

Fortunately for you, he already helped in the best possible way. He freed you from having to do everything absolutely right because he accepted his Son's sacrifice on your behalf. He knows you can't come to salvation all on your own. Decisions don't come easily, though. Choices are constantly coming up, and the battle rages between keeping you on the path or pulling you off the path.

> *P*ractice making the right little decisions today so that you will make the right big decisions tomorrow.

C. S. Lewis said, "Good and evil both increase at compound interest. That is why the little decisions you and I make every day are of such infinite importance." Be aware today of all the choices you make, seek God's help, and offer your options to him. He'll help you move forward with wisdom to achieve his purposes.

Renewed for a Purpose

Lord, be with me in the choices and decisions I make today. Help me move ahead only when I hear your affirmation for what I choose. Amen.

The One and Only Mediator

*There is one God and one mediator between God
and humanity, the human Christ Jesus, who gave himself
as a payment to set all people free.*

—1 Timothy 2:5-6

Timothy tells us here that Christ himself is our mediator with God. He stepped in on our behalf to negotiate a place for us in Heaven. As John Calvin put it, "Christ's work as Mediator was unique: it was to restore us to divine favor and to make us sons [and daughters] of God, instead of sons of men. We became heirs to a heavenly kingdom."

So, okay, you may not stop to realize your life is on trial or that you need someone to go stand in the gaps, but the truth is you do. We all do, because God alone is Holy. We're on a finite path and only God himself could devise a way to bring us back home again from this journey. That's the work God did through our Mediator, Jesus.

Today, let's give thanks for our path and remember the one who gives us life . . . life eternal. Then, let's step out in faith and see what we can do to encourage a few more of God's children to step into the fold. Bring a little bit of heaven to everyone you meet today.

> *E*ncourage others to step out in faith and then labor together to bring heaven to earth.

Renewed for a Purpose

Lord, I thank you for the great sacrifice you made on my behalf. I thank you for loving me before I was even born. Thank you for the great Mediator, our one and only way back to you . . . Jesus Christ. Amen.